The Ketogenic Cookbook

200+ Recipes Ideas to heal your body and Lose Weight (Keto cookbook, Keto Bread, Keto Chaffle and Keto smoothies)

By

Sophia Young

Table of Contents

KETO CHAFFLE RECIPES 190

Introduction

Ketogenic refers to a low-carbohydrate diet. The aim is to eat more calories from fat and protein while eating fewer calories from carbohydrates. The carbohydrates that are easiest to digest, such as starch, pastries, soda, and white bread, are the first to go. When you consume fewer than 50 g of carbohydrates a day, your body easily runs out of energy. This normally takes three or four days. Then you'll begin to break down fat and protein for energy, potentially resulting in weight loss. Ketosis is the term for this state. It's crucial to remember that the ketogenic diet is a short-term diet designed to help you lose weight rather than change your lifestyle. A ketogenic diet is more often used to reduce weight, although it may also be used to treat medical problems such as epilepsy. It can even benefit those suffering from heart failure, some brain disorders, and even acne, although further study is required. Since the keto diet contains too much fat, adherents must ingest fat at every meal time. In a normal 2K-calorie diet, that would seem like 165 g of fat, 40 g of carbohydrates, and 75 g of protein. The exact ratio, on the other hand, is determined by your basic requirements. Nuts (walnuts, almonds), avocados, seeds, olive oil and tofu are among the healthier unsaturated fats allowed on the keto diet. However, oils (coconut, palm), butter, lard, and peanut butter all contain high amounts of saturated fats. Protein is an essential aspect of the keto diet, although it is also difficult to discern between protein items that are lean and protein products rich in fat(saturated), such as beef, bacon, and pork. What for fruits and vegetables? While fruits are generally rich in carbohydrates, unique fruits may be obtained in limited quantities (generally berries) Leafy greens (like kale, chard, Swiss chard, and spinach), broccoli, cauliflower, asparagus, tomatoes, brussels sprouts, bell peppers, garlic, cucumbers, mushrooms, summer squashes, as well as celery are also rich in carbohydrates. One cup of sliced broccoli includes about six carbohydrates. At the same time, there are several possible keto hazards, such as liver deficiency, liver complications, constipation, kidney disorders, and so on. As a result, we can also keep our Keto diet portions in check.

Chapter 1: Understanding The Ketogenic Diet

This chapter delves into the Ketogenic diet in depth. The chapter further discusses which foods to consume on the Keto diet and which foods to stop while on this diet. The Keto diet is often explained in-depth, including how it functions and what health advantages it provides.

The ketogenic diet (or keto diet) is a high-fat, low-carbohydrate diet with various health benefits. Evidently, more than 20 studies suggest that this form of diet will help you lose weight and boost your wellbeing. Diabetes patients, epilepsy patients, patients suffering from Alzheimer's disease, as well as cancer can all benefit from ketogenic diets.

1.1 What is Keto?

The ketogenic diet is a very low carbohydrate, high-fat diet that has a lot in common with the Atkins diet and other low-carb diets. It necessitates a significant reduction of carbohydrate consumption and a replacement with fat. This reduction of carbohydrates puts the body into a metabolic condition known as ketosis. As this occurs, the body's energy production of fat-burning skyrockets. In addition, it converts fat into ketones in the liver, which will supply energy to the brain. Ketogenic diets can result in substantial reductions in insulin as well as blood sugar levels. This, along with the increased ketones, has numerous health benefits.

Ketogenic Diets Come in Many Forms

There are a few variations of the ketogenic diet, including:

The traditional ketogenic diet consists of a diet that is low in carbs, mild in protein, and strong in fats. It usually has a 75 percent fat content, a 5% carbohydrate content, and a 20% protein content.

The cyclic ketogenic diet entails high-carb reefed cycles, such as five ketogenic days accompanied by two days of high carbohydrate use.

A ketogenic diet with particular goals: The diet requires carbs to be inserted in between exercises.

Protein-rich ketogenic diet: This is comparable to a normal keto diet, but it contains extra protein. Usually, the ratio is 60 percent fat, 5% sugars, and 35 percent protein.

However, only normal and protein-rich ketogenic diets have been extensively studied. More complex keto diets, such as targeted or cyclic keto, are mainly utilized by bodybuilders and athletes.

Ketogenic Diet Health Benefits

In fact, the keto diet first gained popularity as a means of treating neurological conditions, such as epilepsy. Following that, research has shown that diet can help with a broad variety of health issues:

Heart disease: The keto diet has been found to decrease risk factors such as body fat, blood sugar, HDL cholesterol and blood pressure.

Alzheimer's disease: The ketogenic diet can ease Alzheimer's symptoms while still delaying the disease's progression.

Epilepsy: Research has demonstrated that a ketogenic diet can significantly reduce seizures in children with epileptic seizures.

Cancer: The diet is actually being used to control a number of diseases and to delay tumor development.

Acne: Lower insulin levels, as well as less sugar or fried food diets, will aid acne recovery.

Parkinson's disease: According to one report, diet can help relieve the effects of Parkinson's disease.

Brain injuries: One study found that the diet would also increase concussions and improve recovery after a brain injury.

Polycystic ovary syndrome: A ketogenic diet may help lower insulin levels and can be helpful in the treatment of polycystic ovary syndrome.

What foods can you consume on a ketogenic diet?

The majority of your meals will revolve around the following foods:

- Salmon, mackerel and tuna are representations of fatty fish.
- Look for pastured eggs, whole eggs, or omega-3 eggs.
- Seek for grass-fed butter plus cream wherever possible.
- Red meat, ham, sausage, turkey, bacon, chicken and steak are all examples of meat.
- Non-processed cheese (goat, cheddar, mozzarella, blue, or cream).
- Flax seeds, walnuts, almonds, pumpkin seeds, chia seeds and other nuts and beans
- Avocado oil, olive oil and coconut oil are the other safe oils.
- Salt, spices and pepper, as well as a variety of herbs, may be used as condiments.
- Avocados: entire avocados or guacamole made freshly.
- Low-carb vegetables including greens, tomatoes, onions, peppers and other related veggies.

Foods to avoid on a ketogenic diet include:

Carbohydrate-rich diets can be avoided as much as possible.

The following is a selection of items that must be eliminated or reduced on a ketogenic diet:

- Sugary drink, ice cream, soda, smoothies, cake, candy and other sugary items
- Wheat, pasta, cereals, rice, and other wheat-based products are examples of starches or grains.
- Sweet potatoes, parsnips, parsnips, potatoes, carrots and other tubers & root vegetables
- Reduced-calorie or low-fat foods are extremely processed and abundant in carbohydrates.
- Fruit: All fruits, with the exception of tiny bits of berries like strawberries.
- Chickpeas, lentils, peas, kidney beans, and other legumes or beans
- Some sauces/condiments: They are also high in unhealthy fat and sugar.

- Unhealthy fats: Limit the intake to mayonnaise, processed vegetable oils, and other processed fats.
- Alcohol: Because of their carb content, certain alcoholic beverages will shake you out of ketosis.
- Dietary ingredients that are sugar-free: Alcohols, which are often rich in sugar, may influence ketone levels in certain situations. These objects seem to have passed through a lot of refining as well.

1.2 **What is the Keto diet, and how does it work?**

The "ketogenic" keto diet consists of consuming a moderate level of protein, a heavy amount of fat, and relatively little carbohydrates; also, the fruit is forbidden. As for every diet fad, the advantages to adherents include improved vitality, weight reduction, and mental clarity. Is the ketogenic diet, though, what it's cracked up to be?

Dietitians and nutritionists are quiet on the topic. Low-carb diets like keto appear to assist with weight loss in the short term, but they are no more successful than any other self-help or conventional diet. They still don't seem to be enhancing athletic results.

The ketogenic diet was created to treat epilepsy instead of losing weight. In the 1920s, physicians found that holding people on low-carb diets induced their bodies to use fat as the predominant fuel source rather than glucose. When only fat is available for the body to combust or burn, the body converts fats to fatty acids, which are then converted to ketones, which can be used and taken up to power the body's cells.

Currently, feeding the body exclusively ketones prevents epilepsy for unclear causes. However, with the advent of anti-seizure medicines, few patients with epilepsy rely on ketogenic diets anymore, while certain people who may not respond to medications may benefit. Low carb diets like the Atkins diet, which gained popularity in the early 2000s, also spawned keto diets for weight loss. In comparison, all groups of meatier-meal diets restrict carbohydrates. This diet does not have a set structure, although most routines provide for fewer than fifty grams of carbs per day.

A keto diet causes the body to enter a state known as ketosis, in which the body's cells become completely reliant on ketones for nutrition. It's not exactly clear that this leads to weight loss, but ketosis decreases appetite and can affect hunger-controlling hormones, including insulin. As a consequence, proteins and fats can keep humans fuller longer than sugars, resulting in lower net calorie intake.

In one head-to-head comparison, researchers looked at 48 separate diet trials in which subjects were randomly allocated to one of the well-known diets. Low-carb diets like South Beach, Atkins, and Zone, as well as low-fat diets like Ornish diets and portion restriction diets like Weight Watchers and Jenny Craig, were among the options.

Every diet resulted in greater weight loss than almost no diet after six months, according to the results. Low-carb and low-fat dieters lost almost equal amounts of weight as compared to non-dieters, with low-carb dieters losing 19 pounds on average versus low-fat dieters dropping 17.6 pounds (7.99 kilograms). At 12 months, both diet styles displayed symptoms of dropping off, with low-fat and low-carb dieters being 16 pounds (7.27 kg) smaller on average than non-dieters.

There were few differences in weight reduction within the diets of designated people. This is in line with the practice of recommending every diet that an individual practice in order to lose weight.

Another study of well-known diets discovered the Atkins diet, which results in greater weight loss than merely teaching people about portion control. Nevertheless, several of the scientific researched about this low-carb diet featured licensed dietitians assisting respondents in making food decisions, rather than the self-directed approach used by most people. This has been seen in other diet studies, according to the researchers, and the tests' results seem to be more positive in the real world than the weight loss.

Finally, a simple comparison between low-carb versus low-fat dieting revealed that there was a statistically significant difference in the amount of weight lost over a year. Low-carbohydrate dieters dropped an average of 13 pounds (6 kg), compared to 11.7 pounds for low-fat dieters (5.3 kg).

Ketogenic diets may help us lose weight, but they are no more successful than other diet methods. Since carbohydrate reserves in the body comprise water molecules, the bulk of the weight lost during the early stages of a ketogenic diet is water weight. This gives the scale an exciting amount at first, but weight reduction slows down with time.

What are the keto effects, and how can they help?

The advantages of a keto diet are close to that of other high-fat, low-carb diets, but it tends to be more successful than centrist low-carb diets. Keto is a low-carb, high-fat diet that maximizes health benefits. However, it will slightly raise the likelihood of complications.

Aid in weight loss

Weight reduction can be improved by converting the body into a fat-burning device. Insulin levels – the hormone that retains fat – are falling rapidly, suggesting that fat burning has risen dramatically. This seems to make it much easier to lose bodyweight without going hungry.

More than thirty high-quality observational studies show that low-carb and keto diets are more effective than other diets at losing weight.

Reverse type 2 diabetes by regulating blood sugar

A ketogenic diet has been shown in research to be successful in the treatment of type 2 diabetes, with total disease reversal occurring in certain instances. It makes perfect sense since keto removes the need for therapy, lowers blood sugar levels, and eliminates the potential negative consequences of high insulin levels.

Since a keto diet will reverse type 2 diabetes, it is likely to be helpful in preventing and reversing pre-diabetes. Keep in mind that "reversal" in this context refers to changing the disease, improving glucose tolerance, and reducing the need for care. It may be so drastically altered that after therapy, blood pressure returns to normal with time. In this context, reversal refers to progressing or deteriorating in the reverse direction of the condition. Changes in your lifestyle, on the other side, just succeed if you bring them into effect. If a person returns to the way of life he or she has before diabetes type 2 appeared and advanced, it is possible that success would return with time.

Improve your mental and physical performance:
Some people use ketogenic diets to boost their mental performance. It's also normal for people to feel more energized while they're in ketosis.
They don't need nutritional carbs for the brain on keto. It runs on ketones 24 hours a day, seven days a week, with a small amount of glucose synthesized in the liver. Carbohydrates are not necessary for the diet. As a result, ketosis leads to a steady flow of food (ketones) to the brain, avoiding significant blood sugar spikes. This will also assist with improved focus and attention, as well as clearing brain fog and improving mental awareness.

Epilepsy Treatment

The keto diet has been used to manage epilepsy since the 19th and 20th centuries and has proved to be effective. It has historically been used mainly for adolescents, although in recent years, it has also proved to be useful to adults. Or, used in conjunction with a keto diet, certain people with epilepsy might be able to take less to no anti-epileptic drugs while being seizure-free. This may help to reduce the drug's adverse effects while still improving cognitive capacity.

Breakfast, Lunch and Dinner Recipes

1 Hot Chocolate

(Ready in about 10 minutes | Serving 1 | Difficulty: Easy)

Per serving: Kcal 173, Fat: 17g, Net Carbs: 5g, Protein: 3g

Ingredients

- 2 tbsp cocoa powder, unsweetened, plus extra for garnish
- 1/4 tsp. of vanilla extract
- 1 1/4 cup of water
- 2 1/2 tsp of keto sugar
- 1/4 cup of heavy cream
- Whipped cream

Instructions

Add cocoa and sugar to a frying pan over moderate flame and whisk. Add 2tbsp water and increase the flame. Add rest of water plus cream and whisk frequently. Add vanilla and stir. Pour mixture in mug and top with whipped cream. Sprinkle cocoa powder and enjoy.

2 Classic bacon with eggs

(Ready in about 10 minutes | Serving 4 | Difficulty: Easy)

Per serving: Kcal 425, Fat: 31g, Net Carbs: 2g, Protein: 33g

Ingredients

- 8 eggs
- cherry tomatoes
- 9 oz. bacon, sliced
- fresh thyme

Instructions

Add bacon to the pan and fry over moderate flame. Add to the plate once it turns crispy and place aside. Fry eggs in the fat left in the pan. Cook to your preference and add tomatoes and cook as well. Add pepper and salt and eat with bacon.

3 keto breakfast

(Ready in about 10 minutes | Serving 1 | Difficulty: Easy)

Per serving: Kcal 424, Fat: 41g, Net Carbs: 1g, Protein: 13g

Ingredients

- 1 cup of baby spinach
- 2 eggs
- 2 tbsp of mayonnaise
- 1 tbsp of butter
- black pepper and salt

Instructions

Warm butter in a pan over moderate flame and add cracked eggs. Cook eggs according to your preference and add pepper and salt over them. Serve with a dollop of mayonnaise plus baby spinach. Have a cup of black coffee along.

4 Spinach and scrambled eggs

(Ready in about 8 minutes | Serving 1 | Difficulty: Easy)

Per serving: Kcal 368, Fat: 32g, Net Carbs: 2g, Protein: 18g

Ingredients

- 1 tbsp of butter
- black pepper and salt
- 2 eggs
- 2 tbsp of whipping cream
- 1 cup of baby spinach
- 1 oz. salmon smoked

Instructions

Warm butter in a pan over moderate flame and fry baby spinach until it turns soft. Add cream and cook until it bubbles and turns creamy. Breaks eggs into the pan and mix to incorporate all the ingredients. Season using pepper and salt. Continue stirring and cook according to your preference. Add eggs to the pan and serve with smoked salmon.

5 Oven pancake

(Ready in about 40 minutes | Serving 4 | Difficulty: Moderate)

Per serving: Kcal 553, Fat: 49g, Net Carbs: 5g, Protein: 22g

Ingredients

- 31/2 oz. pork bacon
- 2 tbsp of butter 4 eggs
- 1 tsp of baking powder
- 2 oz. of yellow onion
- 1 cup of whipping cream
- 1/2 cup of almond flour
- 1/2 cup cottage cheese
- 1 tbsp of husk powder
- 1 tsp of salt

Instructions

Preheat the oven to 350 degrees F. Dice onion and bacon. Warm butter in a pan and cook onion and bacon in the pan until the bacon gets crispy and onion is translucent. Add the rest of the ingredients to a bowl and mix. Pour mixture in a pan and top with onions and bacon. Bake for around 25 minutes and enjoy.

6 Pulled Pork

(Ready in about 20 minutes | Serving 1 | Difficulty: Easy)

Per serving: Kcal 153, Fat: 10, Net Carbs: 8g, Protein: 6g

Ingredients

- 2 tbsp of olive oil
- 1/4 tsp of salt
- 2 eggs
- 1 (115g) diced turnip 1/2 tsp paprika
- 1/4 tsp of garlic powder
- 3 halved(50g) Brussels sprouts
- 1/4 tsp of black pepper
- 1 cup of spinach chopped
- 3 ounces of pulled pork
- 2 tbsp diced red onion
- 1 tbsp of parsley chopped

Instructions

Warm oil in a pan over moderate flame. Add spices and turnip and cook for around 5 minutes.

Add the rest of the veggies and cook for around 3 minutes. Add pork and cook for 2 more minutes. Break eggs and cook for around 5 minutes, covered. Season using pepper and salt and top with parsley.

7 Bacon Egg Cups

(Ready in about 30 minutes | Serving 12 | Difficulty: Easy)

Per serving: Kcal 115, Fat: 8g, Net Carbs: 0g, Protein: 9g

Ingredients

- Bacon strips 12
- pepper, to taste
- 12 Big eggs

Instructions

Preheat the oven to 400 degrees F. Spray a muffin tin using cooking spray and place aside. Use one bacon piece for every muffin and form a basket for the egg. Add bacon inside in a way that it covers the sides, and use scissors to remove the extra bacon. Add this to the bottom of the basket and repeat with the rest of the bacon pieces. Bake for around 7 minutes and break an egg in each basket. Bake for another 15 minutes. Season using pepper and enjoy.

8 Granola Clusters

(Ready in about 45 minutes | Serving 8 | Difficulty: Moderate)

Per serving: Kcal 327, Fat: 31.5, Net Carbs: 6g, Protein: 5.5

Ingredients

- 1 cup of pecan halves
- 1/2 cup of almonds
- 1/4 cup of powdered Sweetener
- 1 cup of flaked coconut
- 1/2 cup of pumpkin seeds
- 1/2 cup of butter
- 1/2 tsp of salt
- 1/4 cup of Swerve Brown
- 1/2 tsp of vanilla extract

Instructions

Preheat the oven to 300 degrees F. Use parchment paper to line a baking dish. Combine everything except sweeteners and butter in a blender and blend. Add sweeteners and butter in a pan placed on low flame. Whish until sweeteners are dissolved, and butter melts. Add nut mixture and mix. Pour mixture in a prepared pan in a single layer. Top with parchment paper and bake for around 30 minutes.

9 Crustless Quiche

(Ready in about 35 minutes | Serving 6 | Difficulty: Moderate)

Per serving: Kcal 216, Fat: 17g, Net Carbs: 4g, Protein: 11g

Ingredients

- 1/2 cup of bacon chopped
- 1/4 tsp of black pepper ground
- 1/2 cup of chopped cherry tomatoes
- 1/2 cup of broccoli chopped
- 1/2 tsp of salt
- 1/2 cup of milk
- 2/3 cup mozzarella cheese shredded
- 1/2 cup of half and half
- 5 eggs

Instructions

Preheat the oven to 325 degrees F. Use cooking spray to spray a baking dish and spread tomatoes, broccoli, plus bacon evenly on the dish. Combine the rest of the ingredients in a bowl and pour over veggies. Sprinkle cheese on top and bake for around 25 minutes.

10 Fluffy Eggs

(Ready in about 10 minutes | Serving 4 | Difficulty: Easy)

Per serving: Kcal 281, Fat: 20.2g, Net Carbs: 5.2g, Protein: 19.7g

For Scrambled eggs

- 1 handful of chives
- Black pepper ground
- 4 ounces of goat cheese
- 8 eggs
- 1/2 tsp of kosher salt
- 2 tbsp of butter

Instructions

Dice the chives. Whisk eggs in a bowl and add goat cheese. Add pepper and salt and stir. Warm butter in a pan over moderate flame. Add eggs mixture, and once eggs start to harden, make folds with a spatula by slowly scraping egg sections. Garnish with chives and enjoy.

11 Keto Pancakes

(Ready in about 10 minutes | Serving 4 | Difficulty: Easy)

Per serving: Kcal 395, Fat: 34, Net Carbs: 12g, Protein: 14g

Ingredients

- 1 cup of almond flour
- 1/3 cup unsweetened almond milk
- 2-3 tbsp of sweetener of choice
- 1/4 tsp of salt
- 1/4 cup of coconut flour
- 5 large eggs
- 1 tsp of baking powder gluten-free
- 1 1/2 tsp of vanilla extract
- 1/4 cup of coconut oil
- Berries

Instructions

Add all the ingredients to a bowl and mix. Preheat the griddle to approximately 300 degrees F. Pour a quarter of the mixture onto the griddle and heat for around2 minutes. Flip to cook the other side for 2 minutes as well. Repeat with the remaining mixture and enjoy.

12 Frittata Muffins

(Ready in about 30 minutes | Serving 12 | Difficulty: Easy)

Per serving: Kcal 164, Fat: 14g, Net Carbs: 4g, Protein: 7g

Ingredients

- 4 tbsp of avocado oil
- 3 minced garlic cloves
- 1/2 pound thawed frozen spinach squeezed dry
- 1/2 medium diced onion
- 1/2 pound sliced cremini mushrooms
- 5 ounces of Prosciutto di Parma
- Kosher salt
- 2 tbsp of coconut flour
- 8 Big eggs
- Ground pepper
- 1/4 cup of coconut milk
- 1 cup halved cherry tomatoes

Instructions

Preheat the oven to 375 degrees F. Warm 2 tbsp of avocado oil in a frying pan over moderate flame. Sauté onions until translucent. Add mushrooms and garlic and cook until the moisture from mushrooms evaporates. Season filling using pepper and salt. Transfer to a plate. Beat eggs with the rest of the ingredients in a separate bowl to prepare the batter. Add spinach and mushrooms and mix. Brush muffin tin with remaining avocado oil and use prosciutto to line all cups. Pour frittata batter in every cup and top with diced tomatoes. Bake for around 20 minutes and turn at half point.

13 Bacon Omelet

(Ready in about 32 minutes | Serving 4 | Difficulty: Easy)

Per serving: Kcal 311, Fat: 20g, Net Carbs: 3g, Protein: 17g

Ingredients

- 8 eggs
- 4 cooked bacon slices chopped
- 1 sliced leek
- 2 tbsp of ghee
- Micro greens
- Black pepper ground and sea salt
- Fresh minced chives

Instructions

Neat eggs in a bowl and season using pepper and salt. Melt ghee in a pan over moderate flame. Cook leek for around 5 minutes in the pan and add cooked bacon plus egg mixture in the pan. Cook until it starts to settle and flip to cook the other side for around 3 minutes. Top with chives and micro greens.

14 Brie Frittata

(Ready in about 25minutes | Serving 6 | Difficulty: Easy)

Per serving: Kcal 338, Fat: 27g, Net Carbs: 1.8g, Protein: 18g

Ingredients

- 8 slices chopped bacon
- 1/2 cup of whipping cream
- 8 Big eggs
- 2 minced cloves garlic
- 1/2 tsp of pepper
- 1/2 tsp of salt
- 4 ounces sliced brie

Instructions

Cook bacon in a pan until it turns crispy. Drain on a plate lined with a paper towel. Whisk eggs with the rest of the ingredients plus bacon(two-thirds). Pour mixture in a pan containing bacon grease and cook until egg at edges set up and is somewhat loose in the center. Layer the diced brie on eggs and sprinkle the rest of the bacon. Preheat the broiler to high temperature and position the oven rack in the oven at the second-highest point. Broil for around 5 minutes.

15 Fried Rice

(Ready in about 30 minutes | Serving 4 | Difficulty: Easy)

Per serving: Kcal 108, Fat: 7g, Net Carbs: 21g, Protein: 13g

Ingredients

- 1 diced into florets cauliflower head
- 1 sliced bunch of scallions
- 2 tbsp of coconut oil
- 3 minced garlic cloves
- 2 peeled carrots, diced
- 1 tbsp fresh ginger minced
- 2 diced celery stalks
- 1 cup of frozen peas
- 1 diced bell pepper
- 2 tbsp of rice vinegar
- 2 tsp of Sriracha
- 3 tbsp of soy sauce

Garnishes

- 1 tbsp coconut oil
- Black pepper ground and sea salt
- 4 tbsp scallions sliced
- 4 eggs
- 4 tbsp fresh cilantro chopped
- 4 tsp of sesame seeds

Instructions

Pulse cauliflower in food processor's bowl for around 3 minutes and place aside. Warm oil in a pan and add ginger, scallions and garlic and cook for around 1 minute. Add celery, bell pepper and carrots and cook for around 11 minutes. Add cauliflower rice and cook for 5 additional minutes. Add frozen peas and mix. Add sriracha, rice vinegar and soy sauce and mix. Place aside. Warm oil in a pan and break eggs in it. Cook for around 4 minutes and season using pepper and salt. Top rice with egg and garnish using 1 tbsp cilantro, tsp sesame seeds and 1 tbsp scallions in four plates.

16 Thai Soup

(Ready in about 22 minutes | Serving 6 | Difficulty: Easy)

Per serving: Kcal 323, Fat: 27g, Net Carbs: 7g, Protein: 15g

Ingredients

Main Soup

- 4 Boneless Chicken Thighs skin removed
- 2 tsp of Thai curry paste
- 4 cloves Garlic, crushed
- 14.5 oz of Coconut Milk
- 2 tsp of Fish Sauce
- 1 tsp of Agave nectar
- 3 tsp of Soy Sauce
- 2 Chopped Green Scallions
- 2 inches chopped Minced Ginger

Veggies

- 1/2 cup of sliced cherry tomatoes
- 3 chopped green scallions
- 1/4 cup of chopped cilantro
- 1 lime, juiced

Instructions

Add soup ingredients in an instant pot and close. Cook by pressing the soup button for around 12 minutes under pressure. Release pressure using quick technique and take out chicken shred and add back to the soup. Add vegetables to broth and sear.

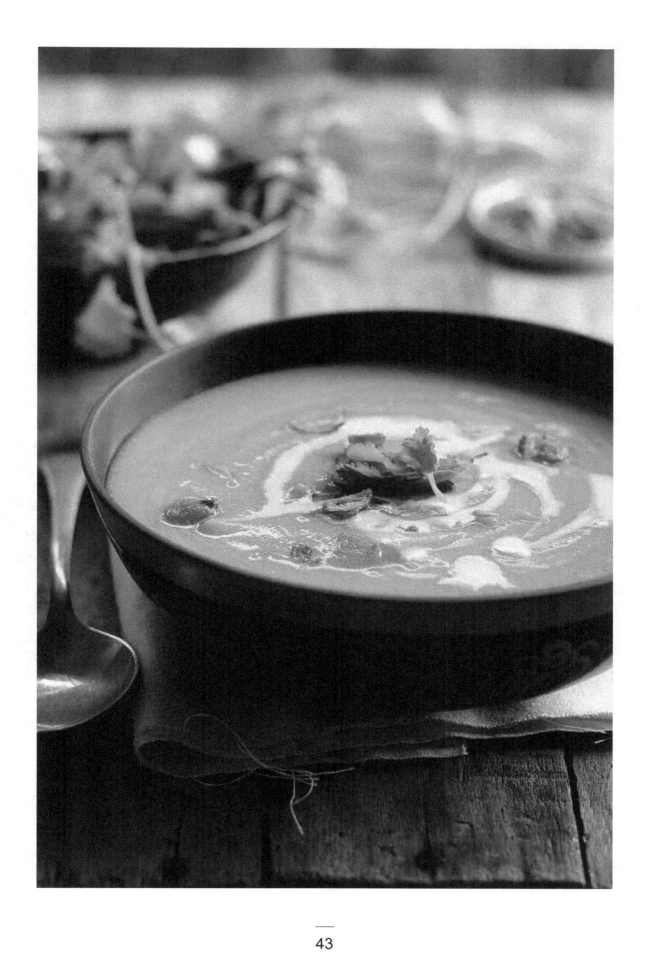

17 Buffalo Soup

(Ready in about 30 minutes | Serving 6 | Difficulty: Easy)

Per serving: Kcal 270, Fat: 16g, Net Carbs: 4g, Protein: 27g

Ingredients

- 1/2 large diced Onion
- 1 tbsp Olive oil
- 1/2 cup diced Celery
- 1 lb cooked shredded chicken
- 4 minced cloves Garlic
- 4 cups of Chicken broth
- 6 oz cubed Cream cheese
- 3 tbsp of Buffalo sauce
- 1/2 cup of half & half

Instructions

Select sauté setting on the instant pot. Add celery, onion and oil. Cook for around 10 minutes. Add garlic and sauté for around one minute. Turn the pot off and add chicken, buffalo sauce and broth. Cover the pot and seal it. Select soup setting and adjust the timer to 5 minutes. After done, release pressure naturally for around 5 minutes and turn to instant release and take the lid off. Ladle around a cup of liquid from the pot and add to the blender without chicken. Add cream cheese and puree. Pour mixture into the pot and add half and half and stir.

18 Jalapeno Soup

(Ready in about 25minutes | Serving 4 | Difficulty: Easy)

Per serving: Kcal 446, Fat: 35g, Net Carbs: 4g, Protein: 28g

Ingredients

- 4 slices of bacon
- 1/2 diced medium onion
- 2 tbsp of butter
- 1/4 cup chopped pickled jalapenos
- 2 cups shredded chicken cooked
- 2 cups of chicken broth
- 4 ounces of cream cheese
- Pepper and salt
- 1 cup sharp cheddar shredded
- 1/3 cup of heavy cream
- 1/4 tsp of garlic powder

Instructions

Fry bacon in a pan until crispy and crumble it and place aside. In the meantime, place the pot over moderate flame and add onion and butter. Saute for around 2 minutes and add half amount of bacon and jalapenos. Add chicken and broth and boil. Then reduce the flame and simmer for around 20 minutes. Add cream cheese to a bowl and microwave for around 20 seconds. Stir and add to soup. Mix heavy cream as well. Add grated cheese and until it is melted, stir. Serve with the rest of the bacon on top.

19 Sausage with Peppers

(Ready in about 2 hours 5 minutes | Serving 6 | Difficulty: Hard)

Per serving: Kcal 313, Fat: 21.7g, Net Carbs: 14g, Protein: 16.4g

Ingredients

- 1 tbsp Olive oil
- 3 diced into strips Bell peppers
- 6 medium Pork links of sausages
- 1 sliced large Onion
- 1/2 tsp of Sea salt
- 1 tbsp of Italian seasoning
- 6 minced cloves Garlic
- 1/4 tsp of Black pepper
- 1 1/2 cups of Marinara sauce

Instructions

Warm oil in a pan over moderate flame. Add sausage and cook for around 2 minutes on each side. Add the rest of the ingredients except marinara in the meantime in a slow cooker. Toss to mix and spread the marinara sauce in a layer on veggies. Add sausage and cook for around 3 hours on a high setting.

20 Beef Barbacoa

(Ready in about 4 hours 10 minutes | Serving 9 | Difficulty: Hard)

Per serving: Kcal 242, Fat: 11g, Net Carbs: 2g, Protein: 32g

Ingredients

- 3 lb trimmed Beef brisket diced into chunks of 2 inch
- 2 Chipotle chiles in adobo medium
- 2 whole Bay leaf
- 1/2 cup of Beef broth
- 5 minced Garlic cloves
- 1 tbsp of Dried oregano
- 2 tbsp of Apple vinegar
- 2 tsp of Sea salt
- 2 tbsp of Lime juice
- 2 tsp of Cumin
- 1 tsp of Black pepper

Instructions

Add all the ingredients except beef plus bay leaves in a blender and puree. You will get a smooth mixture. Add beef to the slow cooker and pour blender mixture on it. Add bay leaves and cook for 6 hours at the high setting.

21 Cauliflower Shrimp

(Ready in about 30 minutes | Serving 2 | Difficulty: Easy)

Per serving: Kcal 302, Fat: 18g, Net Carbs: 13g, Protein: 24g

Spicy Shrimp

- 1 tbsp of paprika
- 1 pound deveined shrimp peeled
- 2 tsp of garlic powder
- 1 tbsp of olive oil
- 1/2tsp of cayenne pepper
- Black pepper ground and salt

Cauliflower Grits

- 1 tbsp of unsalted butter
- 1 cup of whole milk
- 4 cups of riced cauliflower
- 1/2 cup of crumbled goat cheese
- Black pepper ground and salt

Garlic Arugula

- 1 tbsp of extra-virgin olive oil
- 4 cups of baby arugula
- 3 sliced garlic cloves
- Black pepper ground and salt

Instructions

Mix cayenne, paprika and garlic powder in a bowl. Add shrimp to a sealable bag and add the mixture in it. Toss and refrigerate the bag. Melt butter in a pot over moderate flame. Cook cauliflower rice for around 3minutes. Add half amount of milk and simmer for around 8 minutes. Add rest of milk and simmer for around 10 minutes. Add goat cheese and season using pepper and salt. Warm 1 tbsp oil in a pan for garlic arugula. Sauté garlic for around 1 minute. Add arugula and sauté for around 4minutes. Season using pepper and salt and take out on a plate. Add the rest of the olive oil in this pan and sauté shrimp for around 5 minutes. Season using pepper and salt. Divide grits equally among 4 plates and top with a quarter amount of each shrimp and arugula.

22 Cheese Spinach

(Ready in about 10 minutes | Serving 4 | Difficulty: Easy)

Per serving: Kcal 166, Fat: 15.1, Net Carbs: 1.7, Protein: 4.4

Ingredients

- 1 tbsp butter, room temperature
- 1 clove garlic, minced
- 10 ounces spinach
- 1/2 tsp garlic salt
- 1/4 tsp ground black pepper, or more to taste
- 1/2tsp cayenne pepper
- 3 ounces cream cheese
- 1/2 cup double cream

Instructions

Add butter to a pan and melt over moderate flame. Cook garlic for around 30 seconds and add spinach. Cook for around 2 minutes, covered. Season with cayenne, pepper and salt. Add cream and cheese and cook until it melts.

23 Tangy Chicken Drumettes

(Ready in about 40 minutes | Serving 4 | Difficulty: Moderate)

Per serving: Kcal 209, Fat: 12.2g, Net Carbs: 0.4, Protein: 23.2g

Ingredients

- 1 pound chicken drumettes
- 1 tbsp olive oil
- 2 tbsp butter, melted
- 1garlic cloves, sliced
- Fresh juice of 1/2 lemon
- 2 tbsp white wine
- Salt and ground black pepper, to taste
- 1 tbsp fresh scallions, chopped

Instructions

Preheat the oven to 440 degrees F. Line a pan using parchment paper and add chicken. Drizzle with butter and oil. Add the rest of the ingredients and bake for around 35 minutes. Garnish with scallions.

24 Ranch Chicken

(Ready in about 20 minutes | Serving 4 | Difficulty: Easy)

Per serving: Kcal 295, Fat: 19.5g, Net Carbs: 2.9g, Protein: 3.1g

Ingredients

- 2 chicken breasts
- 2 tbsp butter, melted
- 1 tsp salt
- 1/2 tsp garlic powder
- 1/2 tsp cayenne pepper
- 1/2 tsp black peppercorns, crushed
- 1/2 tbsp ranch seasoning mix
- 4 ounces Ricotta cheese, room temperature
- 1/2 cup Monterey-Jack cheese, grated
- 4 slices bacon, chopped
- 1/4 cup scallions, chopped

Instructions

Preheat the oven to 370 degrees F. Drizzle butter over chicken. Add seasonings to chicken and cook chicken in the pan for around 5 minutes on each side. Coat a baking dish and add chicken. Add bacon and cheese and bake for around 12 minutes. Add scallions on top.

25 Garlic Chicken Wings

(Ready in about 25 minutes | Serving 4 | Difficulty: Easy)

Per serving: Kcal 131, Fat: 7.8g, Net Carbs: 1.8g, Protein: 13.4g

Ingredients

- 8 chicken wings
- 2 tbsp ghee, melted

The Marinade

- 2 garlic cloves, minced
- 1/4 cup leeks, chopped
- 2 tbsp lemon juice
- Salt and ground black pepper, to taste
- 1/2 tsp paprika
- 1 tsp dried rosemary

Instructions

Add marinade ingredients in a bowl and coat chicken with it. Cover and leave for around1 an hour. Preheat the grill to moderate temperature. Drizzle chicken with melted ghee and grill for around 20 minutes.

26 Steak Salad

(Ready in about 20 minutes | Serving 4 | Difficulty: Easy)

Per serving: Kcal 231, Fat: 17g, Net Carbs: 6g, Protein: 13.8g

Ingredients

- 2 tbsp olive oil
- 8 ounces flank steak, salt-and-pepper-seasoned
- 1cucumber, sliced
- 1/2 cup onions, finely sliced
- 1 ripe avocado, peeled and sliced
- 2 medium-sized heirloom tomatoes, sliced
- 2 ounces baby arugula
- 1 tbsp fresh coriander, chopped
- 3 tbsp lime juice

Instructions

Warm 1 tbsp oil in a pan over moderate flame and cook steak for around 5 minutes. Transfer steak to bowl and add rest of ingredients. Drizzle the rest of the oil and lime juice and eat after chilling.

27 Catfish

(Ready in about 25 minutes | Serving 4 | Difficulty: Easy)

Per serving: Kcal 510, Fat: 40g, Net Carbs: 5.5g, Protein: 31.3g

Ingredients

- 1 tbsp of sesame oil
- 4 scallions
- 11 ounces of cauliflower
- 2 ounces of butter
- 1 minced garlic clove
- Black pepper ground and salt
- 1 tspgrated ginger root
- Cayenne pepper
- 1 sprig crushed rosemary
- 2 sprigs crushed dried thyme
- 24 ounces of catfish
- 1/2 cup of double cream
- 1/2 cup of cream cheese
- 1 egg

Instructions

Preheat the oven to around 390 degrees F. Spray casserole dish using cooking spray. Add oil to pan and warm over moderate flame. Cook scallions and cauliflower for around 5 minutes. Add ginger and garlic and cook for one more minute. Transfer veggies to the dish and sprinkle using seasonings. Top with catfish. Mix cream, cheese and egg in a bowl and spread over casserole. Add butter slices on top and bake for around 22 minutes.

28 Salad- Swedish Style

(Ready in about 8 minutes | Serving 3 | Difficulty: Easy)

Per serving: Kcal 134, Fat: 7.9g, Net Carbs: 5.4g, Protein: 10.2g

Ingredients

- 1/2 cup of baby spinach
- 6 ounces of flaked herring pieces pickled
- 2tbspof basil leaves
- 1 chopped bell pepper
- 2 tbspof chopped fresh chives
- Black pepper ground and salt
- 1 tsp of minced garlic
- 1 chopped red onion
- 2 tbspof freshly squeezed lime juice

Instructions

Add veggies to a bowl and mix. Drizzle lime juice and sprinkle using pepper and salt. Toss and enjoy your salad.

29 Fish Medley

(Ready in about 20 minutes | Serving 4 | Difficulty: Easy)

Per serving: Kcal 151, Fat: 3g, Net Carbs: 5.8, Protein: 24.4g

Ingredients

- 1 tsp sesame oil
- 1/2 cup scallions, thinly sliced
- 1/2 tsp fresh ginger, grated
- 1/2 tsp garlic, crushed
- 1 tsp red curry paste
- 2 whole star anise
- 1 tsp smoked paprika
- 2 ripe tomatoes, crushed
- Ground black pepper and sea salt
- 1 pound snapper, cut into bite-sized pieces

Instructions

Add oil to a pot and warm over moderate flame. Add ginger and scallions and cook for around 1 minute. Add the rest of the ingredients and reduce the flame. Simmer for around 15 minutes and enjoy.

30 Ham Wraps

(Ready in about 10 minutes | Serving 3 | Difficulty: Easy)

Per serving: Kcal 308, Fat: 19.9g, Net Carbs: 4.3g, Protein: 27.8g

Ingredients

- 1/2 cup dry white wine
- 1/2 cup water
- 1/2 tsp mixed peppercorns
- 1/2 tsp dry mustard powder
- 1/2 pound ahi tuna steak
- 6 slices of ham
- 1/2Hass avocado, peeled, pitted and sliced
- 1 tbsp fresh lemon juice6 lettuce leaves

Instructions

Add all the ingredients except lemon and avocado in a bowl and mix. Add to pan with tuna and simmer for around 5 minutes on each side. Slice the tuna after removing the liquid. Drizzle lemon over and add avocado. Roll wraps and place on a lettuce leaf.

31 Alaskan Cod

(Ready in about 10 minutes | Serving 4 | Difficulty: Easy)

Per serving: Kcal 166, Fat: 8.2g, Net Carbs: 2.6g, Protein: 19.8g

Ingredients

- 1 tbsp coconut oil
- 4 Alaskan cod fillets
- Salt and freshly ground black pepper, to taste
- 6 leaves basil, chiffonade
- Mustard Cream Sauce:
- 1 tsp yellow mustard
- 1 tsp paprika
- 1/4 tsp ground bay leaf
- 3 tbsp cream cheese
- 1/2 cup Greek-style yogurt
- 1 garlic clove, minced
- 1 tsp lemon zest
- 1 tbsp fresh parsley, minced
- Sea salt and ground black pepper, to taste

Instructions

Add oil to the pan and warm over moderate flame. Add fish and sear for around 3 minutes on each side. Season using pepper and salt. Add sauce ingredients in a bowl and mix. Top fillets with sauce and garnish with basil leaves.

32 Paprika Omelet

(Ready in about 10 minutes | Serving 2 | Difficulty: Easy)

Per serving: Kcal 287, Fat: 22.6g, Net Carbs: 1.3g, Protein: 19.8g

Ingredients

- 2 tsp ghee, room temperature
- 4 eggs, whisked
- 4 tbsp goat cheese
- 1tsp paprika
- Sea salt and ground black pepper, to taste

Instructions

Add ghee to the pan and melt over moderate flame. Whisk eggs in a bowl and add to the pan. Cover the pan and reduce the flame to a low temperature. Cook for around 4 minutes. Add paprika and cheese and cook for 3 more minutes. Season using pepper and salt.

33 Boiled Eggs

(Ready in about 10 minutes | Serving 3 | Difficulty: Easy)

Per serving: Kcal 222, Fat: 17.6g, Net Carbs: 5.7g, Protein: 12.2

Ingredients

- 6 eggs
- 1/2 tsp kosher salt
- 1/2 tsp ground black pepper
- 1/2 tsp cayenne pepper
- 1/2 tsp dried dill weed
- 1 avocado, pitted and sliced
- 1tbsp lemon juice

Instructions

Add water to the pan and boil. Add eggs and cook for around 6 minutes on low heat. Peel eggs and cut them in half. Sprinkle with seasonings and drizzle lemon juice over avocado slices. Serve on the side with eggs.

34 Stuffed Peppers

(Ready in about 45 minutes | Serving 3 | Difficulty: Moderate)

Per serving: Kcal 194, Fat: 13.9g, Net Carbs: 3.5g, Protein: 13.3

Ingredients

- 3 bell peppers, halved, seeds removed
- 3 eggs, whisked
- 1 cup Mexican cheese blend
- 1 tsp chili powder
- 1 garlic clove, minced
- 1 tsp onion powder
- 1ripe tomato, pureed
- 1 tsp mustard powder

Instructions

Preheat the oven to 370 degrees F. Add oil to the pan and combine eggs, chili powder, cheese, onion powder and garlic in a bowl. Divide filling equally among bell peppers. Mix mustard powder and tomatoes and pour in pan. Bake for around 40 minutes, covered with foil

35 Kale Bake

(Ready in about 35 minutes | Serving 4 | Difficulty: Moderate)

Per serving: Kcal 384, Fat: 29.1g, Net Carbs: 5.9g, Protein: 25.1g

Ingredients

- Nonstick cooking spray
- 6 ounces kale, torn into pieces
- 4 eggs, whisked
- 1 cup Cheddar cheese, grated
- 1 cup Romano cheese
- 2 tbsp sour cream
- 1 garlic clove, minced
- Sea salt, to taste
- 1/2 tsp ground black pepper, or more to taste
- 1/2 tsp cayenne pepper

Instructions

Preheat the oven to 365 degrees F. Spray pan using cooking spray and mix everything in a bowl. Pour mixture into the prepared pan and bake for around 35 minutes.

36 Cheese Meatballs

(Ready in about 25 minutes | Serving 8 | Difficulty: Easy)

Per serving: Kcal 389, Fat: 31.3g, Net Carbs: 1.6g, Protein: 23.8

Ingredients

- 1/2 pound ground pork
- 1 pound ground turkey
- 1 garlic clove, minced
- 4tbsp pork rinds, crushed
- 2 tbsp shallots, chopped
- 4 ounces mozzarella string cheese, cubed
- 1 ripe tomato, pureed
- Salt and ground black pepper, to taste

Instructions

Combine all the ingredients in a bowl except cheese. Shape eatable balls out of this mixture. Add cheese cube in every ball and line a baking sheet with parchment paper. Place balls on a sheet and bake for around 25 minutes at around 350 degrees F.

37 Italian Crisps

(Ready in about 10 minutes | Serving 4 | Difficulty: Easy)

Per serving: Kcal 134, Fat: 11.1g, Net Carbs: 0.4g, Protein: 4.9g

Ingredients

- 1 cup sharp Cheddar cheese, grated
- 1/4 tsp ground black pepper
- 1/2tsp cayenne pepper
- 1 tsp Italian seasoning

Instructions

Preheat the oven to 400 degrees F and line parchment paper on a baking sheet. Mix everything in a bowl and pour onto a sheet in for of heaps of the size of a tbsp. Bake for around 8 minutes.

38 Spicy Meatballs

(Ready in about 15 minutes | Serving 3 | Difficulty: Easy)

Per serving: Kcal 458, Fat: 35.8g, Net Carbs: 4.3g, Protein: 28.2g

Ingredients

Sauce

- 3 ounces Asiago cheese, grated
- 1/4 cup mayonnaise
- 1 chili pepper, minced
- 1 tsp yellow mustard
- 1 tsp Italian parsley
- 1/2 tsp red pepper flakes, crushed
- 1/2 tsp sea salt
- 1/2 tsp ground black pepper

Meatballs

- 1/2 pound ground beef
- 1 egg
- 1 tbsp olive oil

Instructions

Add all the ingredients in the bowl except egg and beef and mix. Add egg and beef and combine thoroughly. Make meatballs out of the mixture. Warm oil in a pan placed on a moderate flame. Cook each side of meatballs for around 3 minutes.

39 Cheese Stuffed Mushrooms

(Ready in about 25 minutes | Serving 5 | Difficulty: Easy)

Per serving: Kcal 148, Fat: 8.4g, Net Carbs: 4.8g, Protein: 14.1g

Ingredients

- 4 ounces ground beef
- 2 ounces ground pork
- Kosher salt and ground black pepper, to taste
- 1/4 cup goat cheese, crumbled
- 2 tbsp Romano cheese, grated
- 2 tbsp shallot, minced
- 1 garlic clove, minced
- 1 tsp dried basil
- 1/2 tsp dried oregano
- 1/2 tsp dried rosemary
- 20 button mushrooms, stems removed

Instructions

Add everything except mushrooms in a bowl and mix. Stuff this mixture inside mushrooms. Preheat the oven to 370 degrees F. Bake these mushrooms in a pan for around 18 minutes.

40 Beef with Herbs

(Ready in about 50 minutes | Serving 4 | Difficulty: Moderate)

Per serving: Kcal 421, Fat: 35.7g, Net Carbs: 5.9g, Protein: 19.7g

Ingredients

- 1 tbsp olive oil
- 1 pound rib eye, cut into strips
- 2 tbsp rice wine
- 1/4cup beef bone broth
- Sea salt and ground black pepper, to taste
- 2 tbsp fresh parsley, finely chopped
- 2 tbsp fresh chives, finely chopped
- 2chipotle peppers in adobo sauce, chopped
- 1 garlic clove, crushed
- 2 small-sized ripe tomatoes, pureed
- 1 yellow onion, peeled and chopped
- 1/2 tsp dry mustard
- 1 tsp dried basil
- 1 tsp dried marjoram

Instructions

Warm oil in a pan placed on a moderate flame. Sear beef in pan for around 6 minutes. Reduce flame and add the rest of the ingredients and cook for around 40 minutes. Take the beef out and shred and enjoy.

41 Chinese Beef Skillet

(Ready in about 15 minutes | Serving 3 | Difficulty: Easy)

Per serving: Kcal 179, Fat: 10.4g, Net Carbs: 5.8g, Protein: 16.5g

Ingredients

- 1 tbsp sesame oil
- 1/2 pound ground chuck
- 1 shallot, minced
- 1 garlic clove, minced
- 1 (1/2-inch) piece ginger root, peeled and grated
- 1 bell pepper, seeded and sliced
- 4 ounces brown mushrooms, sliced
- 1 tsp tamari soy sauce
- 1 tbsp rice wine
- 2 whole star anise
- Himalayan salt and ground black pepper, to taste

Instructions

Warm oil in a pan over moderate flame and cook chuck until it changed its color. Then cook veggies in drippings inside the pan. Add rest of ingredients and beef to pan. Reduce flame and simmer for around 3 minutes.

42 Beef Stroganoff

(Ready in about 1 hour | Serving 4 | Difficulty: Hard)

Per serving: Kcal 303, Fat: 17.2g, Net Carbs: 5.6g, Protein: 32.4g

Ingredients

- 2 tbsp lard, room temperature
- 1 pound beef stew meat, cut across the grain into strips
- 1/2 yellow onion, peeled and chopped
- 2 garlic cloves, minced
- 4ounces fresh mushrooms, sliced
- 1/2 tsp salt
- 1 tsp smoked paprika
- 1/4tsp black pepper
- 1/2 tsp dried basil
- 1/4 cup red cooking wine
- 4 cups vegetable broth
- 1 fresh tomato, pureed
- 2 celery stalks, chopped
- 1/2 cup sour cream

Instructions

Place stockpot over moderate flame and melt the lard in it. Cook meat until it turns brown. Add garlic and onion and cook for around 1 minute. Add mushrooms, and until they turn tender, cook. Add rest of ingredients except sour cream and seasonings and simmer for around 50 minutes, covered. Add sour cream after turning the heat off and mix.

43 Chicken Zoodles

(Ready in about 19 minutes | Serving 4 | Difficulty: Easy)

Per serving: Kcal 411, Fat: 18.8g, Net Carbs: 11.7g, Protein: 45.7g

Ingredients

- 1/2 tsp of coconut butter
- 500 g of chicken fillets
- 1 medium onion diced
- 1 garlic minced
- Two zucchinis medium
- 400 g tomatoes crushed
- 100 g of raw cashews
- 7-10 chopped cherry tomatoes
- Salt, pepper, basil and oregano

Instructions

Warm pan over moderate flame. Cook butter and onions for around 1 minute. Make 2 cm pieces of chicken. Add garlic and chicken to the pan and sprinkle with seasonings. Cook for around 6 minutes. Spiralize zucchini in the meantime. Add tomatoes(crushed) and simmer for around 5 minutes. Roast cashews using another pan. Season with salt, paprika and turmeric. Add cherry tomatoes, zoodles and season using salt. Cook for another minute. Serve zoodles with fresh basil and cashews.

44 Creamy Tuscan Chicken

(Ready in about 25 minutes | Serving 6 | Difficulty: Easy)

Per serving: Kcal 368, Fat: 25g, Net Carbs: 7g, Protein: 30g

Ingredients

- 11/2 pounds of boneless skinless sliced chicken breasts
- 1 cup of heavy cream
- 1 cup chopped spinach
- 2 Tbsp of olive oil
- 1/2 cup of chicken broth
- 1 tsp of Italian seasoning
- 1 tsp of garlic powder
- 1/2 cup of parmesan cheese
- 1/2 cup of dried tomatoes

Instructions

Warm oil in a pan and cook each side of the chicken for around 5 minutes. Remove and place aside. Add everything except spinach and tomatoes to the pan and whisk over a moderate flame to form a thick mixture. Add tomatoes and spinach and simmer until spinach wilts. Add chicken and heat.

45 Turkey and peppers

(Ready in about 20 minutes | Serving 4 | Difficulty: Easy)

Per serving: Kcal 230, Fat: 8g, Net Carbs: 11g, Protein: 30g

Ingredients

- 1/2 large sliced sweet onion
- 1 pound cut into steaks turkey tenderloin
- 1 diced into strips yellow bell pepper
- 2 tbsp divided olive oil extra-virgin
- 1 diced into strips red bell pepper
- 1 tsp divided salt
- 1/2tsp of Italian seasoning
- 2 tsp of red wine vinegar
- 1/4tsp of ground black pepper
- 1 14-ounce can of crushed tomatoes

Instructions

Sprinkle turkey with half tsp salt. Warm 1 tbsp oil in a pan and cook half of the turkey for around 3 minutes. Transfer to a plate and add remaining oil to the pan. Repeat with the rest of the turkey. Add veggies and half tsp salt to the pan and cook for around 7 minutes. Sprinkle with seasoning plus pepper and cook on a moderate flame for around 30 seconds. Add vinegar and cook for another 20 seconds. Add turkey to the pan and simmer for around 2 minutes. Top with basil and parsley.

46 Butter Chicken

(Ready in about 30 minutes | Serving 6 | Difficulty: Easy)

Per serving: Kcal 293, Fat: 17g, Net Carbs: 9g, Protein: 29g

Ingredients

- 1.5 lbs cubed chicken breast
- 4 oz plain Greek yogurt whole milk
- 3 tsp grated fresh ginger
- 2 tbsp of garam masala
- 3 tsp garlic minced
- 1 tbsp of coconut oil

Sauce

- 2 tbsp of butter
- 2 tsp grated fresh ginger
- 1/2 cup of heavy cream
- 2 tsp garlic minced
- 14.5 oz can tomatoes crushed
- 1 onion
- 1 tbsp coriander ground
- 2 tsp of cumin
- 1/2tbsp of garam masala
- 1 tsp of chili powder
- Salt

Instructions

Dice chicken into pieces of 2 inch and mix with garam masala, 1 tsp each of garlic and ginger in a bowl. Add yogurt and mix. Place in the fridge for around 30 minutes. Add tomatoes, garlic, ginger, spices and onion in a blender and blend to make a smooth mixture. Place aside. Warm 1 tbsp oil in a pan and add marinade and chicken. Cook each side for around 4 minutes. Add sauce and cook for 6 more minutes. Add ghee and heavy cream and cook for an additional minute. Top using cilantro.

47 Asparagus Chicken

(Ready in about 30 minutes | Serving 3 | Difficulty: Easy)

Per serving: Kcal 572, Fat: 31g, Net Carbs: 10g, Protein: 62g

Ingredients

- 3 Breasts Chicken
- 12 Stalks removed Asparagus
- 1 cup of mozzarella shredded
- 1 tsp of Garlic paste
- 1/2 cup of Cream Cheese
- 1 tsp of Olive Oil
- 1 tbsp of Butter
- 3/4 cup of Marinara Sauce
- Pepper and salt

Instructions

Slice chicken without cutting from the center. Cut stalks from asparagus. Rub garlic paste, salt and pepper over chicken and spread with cream cheese. Place 4 asparagus stalks in the center and fold the breasts. Preheat the oven to 400 degrees F and cook each side for around 7 minutes. Top with marinara sauce and mozzarella. Broil for around 5 minutes.

48 Chicken Chili

(Ready in about 30 minutes | Serving 6 | Difficulty: Easy)

Per serving: Kcal 201, Fat: 11g, Net Carbs: 7g, Protein: 18g

Ingredients

- 4 shredded chicken breasts
- 2 cups of Chicken broth
- 1 tbsp of Butter
- 1/2 chopped onion
- 10 oz canned diced tomatoes, undrained
- 4 oz of Cream cheese
- 2 oz of tomato paste
- 1 tbsp of Cumin
- 1 tbsp of Chili powder
- 1/2 tbsp of Garlic powder
- Pepper and salt

Instructions

Boil chicken in broth for around 12 minutes. Take out and shred. Melt butter in a pot over moderate flame and cook the onion for around 2 minutes. Add chicken and rest of the ingredients except cream cheese in pot and stir. Boil and reduce the flame to simmer for around 10 minutes. Cut cream into chunks of 1 inch. Add to pot and stir until mixed. Season using pepper and salt.

49 Taco Avocados

(Ready in about 20 minutes | Serving 6 | Difficulty: Easy)

Per serving: Kcal 401, Fat: 28g, Net Carbs: 5g, Protein: 26g

Ingredients

- 1 pound beef ground
- 1/2 tsp of Salt
- 1 tbsp of Chili Powder
- 1/2 tsp of Dried Oregano
- 3/4 tsp of Cumin
- 1/4 tsp of Garlic Powder
- 4 ounces of tomato sauce
- 1/4 tsp of Onion Powder
- 3 halved avocados
- 1 cup shredded cheddar cheese
- 1/4 cup sliced cherry tomatoes
- 1/4 cup shredded lettuce

Instructions

Add beef to a pan and cook until it turns brown. Remove grease and mix tomato sauce and seasonings. Cook for around 4 minutes and take the pit out of avocados. Load taco meat in crater and top with tomatoes, cheese, sour cream, cilantro and lettuce.

50 Broccoli Beef Bowls

(Ready in about 30 minutes | Serving 4 | Difficulty: Easy)

Per serving: Kcal 388, Fat: 29g, Net Carbs: 14g, Protein: 30g

Ingredients

Beef

- 1 pound grass-fed beef ground
- 1 tsp of granulated garlic
- 1 tsp of fine salt
- 1 tbsp of cooking fat
- 1 tbsp of coconut aminos

Broccoli

- 4 diced into florets broccoli crowns
- 1/2 tsp of fine salt
- 1 tbsp of avocado oil

Sunshine Sauce

- 1 tbsp of cooking fat
- 1/2 of fine salt
- 2 tbsp seed sunflower butter
- 2 tsp of coconut aminos
- 1 tsp of ground ginger
- one lemon, juiced
- 1 minced green onion
- 1/4 cup of bone broth

To assemble

- 4 cups of baby spinach

Instructions

Preheat oven to around 400 degrees F. Mix salt and fat with broccoli on pan and massage fat into florets. Cook for around 20 minutes. Crumble beef in a pan and add garlic and salt. Stir and add coconut aminos and turn flame to high. Cook until beef turns crispy and brown. Place a pot on moderate flame and melt fat in it. Add seed butter and sunflower and stir to make a smooth mixture. Add rest of ingredients except lemon juice and stir. Take off the heat and mix lemon juice. Add baby spinach to 4 bowls and divide beef equally. Add broccoli florets and top with sauce.

51 Cauliflower-Bacon Cheese Mash

(Ready in about 15 minutes | Serving 4 | Difficulty: Easy)

Per serving: Kcal 399, Fat: 32.2g, Sodium 877.8mg, Protein: 18.8g

Ingredients

- 1 cauliflower, large head, diced into florets
- ½ lb. bacon, diced
- 1 cup of Parmesan cheese, shredded
- 2 tbsp. medium-chain triglyceride oil
- 4 tbsp. unsalted butter
- Sea salt to taste
- ½ tbsp. apple cider vinegar

Instruction

- Cook the bacon in a big skillet over the medium-high flame, sometimes flipping, for five to ten minutes or evenly browned. Reserve the grease in the skillet and drain on the paper towels.
- In a pressure cooker, place the cauliflower in a metal or silicone steamer basket. Fill the container with 1 cup of water. Cover the lid and lock it. Set the timer for four minutes and select the Steam function. Allow for a ten to a fifteen-minute build-up of pressure.
- Pressure can be released slowly and cautiously using the quick-release system according to the manufacturer's directions, which should take around five minutes. Remove the lid by unlocking it.
- Drain the cauliflower and put it in a big mixing bowl. Combine the Parmesan cheese, butter, MCT oil, vinegar, and salt in a mixing bowl. Using an immersion blender, blend until absolutely smooth. Add the sliced bacon and mix properly. Add one or two teaspoons of the bacon grease that has been put aside.

52 Spaghetti Squash With Blue Cheese And Bacon

(Ready in about 15 minutes | Serving 2 | Difficulty: Easy)

Per serving: Kcal 339, Fat: 24.3g, Sodium 691.2mg, Protein: 13.5g

Ingredients

- 1 tbsp. olive oil
- 1 spaghetti squash, small
- Ground black pepper and salt according to taste
- 2 tbsp. crumbled blue cheese
- 1 (4 oz.) sliced package mushrooms
- 4 slices bacon, diced into 1/2-inch pieces
- 1 clove minced garlic
- ¼ cup of sour cream
- 2 cup of baby spinach

Instruction

- Preheat oven to 400 degrees Fahrenheit. Aluminum foil can be used to line a baking sheet.
- Using a sharp knife, cut the stem from the end of the spaghetti squash. Squash can be cut in half lengthwise, and the seeds scraped off. Brush with olive oil and season with salt and pepper.
- Bake for forty-five minutes in a preheated oven till tender. Remove the fried flesh to a bowl and put it aside. Return the shells of the spaghetti squash to the baking sheet.
- Cook the bacon in a big skillet over medium-high flame, sometimes flipping, for five to six minutes, or till evenly browned. On paper towels, drain the bacon slices.
- Cook for four to five minutes with the garlic and mushrooms in the skillet. In a large mixing bowl, combine the spinach and cooked bacon. Stir for two to three minutes or till spinach is wilted. Toss the mushroom mixture into the squash bowl. Combine the salt, pepper, and sour cream in a mixing bowl. Stir until all of the fillings are distributed.

- Fill the squash shells with the filling. On each half, sprinkle 1 tbsp. blue cheese. Return to oven and bake for another four to five minutes, or till the cheese has melted and the squash has cooked through.

53 Ranch Cauliflower Crackers

(Ready in about 20 minutes | Serving 18 | Difficulty: Easy)

Per serving: Kcal 29, Fat: 1.5g, Sodium 103.5mg, Protein: 2.5g

Ingredients

- Cheesecloth
- 1 (12 oz.) frozen riced cauliflower
- 1 cup of Parmesan cheese, shredded
- 1 egg
- ⅛ tsp. cayenne pepper, or according to taste
- 1 tbsp. salad dressing mix, dry ranch

Instructions

- In a microwave-safe bowl, put the riced cauliflower. Microwave for three to four minutes, covered. Allow it to cool for fifteen minutes in a strainer lined with cheesecloth. Squeeze the moisture out of the riced cauliflower after it has cooled.
- Preheat oven to 425 degrees Fahrenheit. Using parchment paper, line the baking dish.
- In a mixing bowl, combine the egg, riced cauliflower, cayenne pepper, and ranch blend. Stir in the Parmesan cheese till it is fully incorporated.
- With a tiny cookie scoop, transfer the mixture onto a prepared cookie sheet and flatten it to around 1/16-inch thickness with a tiny hand-rolling pin, cup, or your hand. The crispier your cracker is, the thinner the dough will be.
- Bake for ten minutes in a preheated oven, then flip and bake for another ten minutes. Allow cooling on a wire shelf.

54 Easy Cauliflower Casserole

(Ready in about 10 minutes | Serving 2 | Difficulty: Easy)

Per serving: Kcal 469, Fat: 40.9g, Sodium 494.1mg, Protein: 18.1g

Ingredients

- 1 cup of Cheddar cheese, shredded
- ½ head cauliflower florets
- 1 pinch freshly ground black pepper and salt or according to taste
- ½ cup of heavy cream

Instruction

- Preheat oven to 400 degrees Fahrenheit.
- Cook the cauliflower in a big pot of lightly salted water until soft yet firm to the bite, approximately ten minutes. Drain.
- In a big mixing bowl, combine the cream, Cheddar cheese, pepper, and salt. Cover cauliflower with the cheese mixture in a casserole dish.
- Bake for twenty-five minutes in a preheated oven till the cheese is golden brown and bubbly.

55 White Chicken Chili

(Ready in about 20 minutes | Serving 8 | Difficulty: Easy)

Per serving: Kcal 591, Fat: 49.6g, Sodium 795mg, Protein: 31.8g

Ingredients

- 1 stick divide butter
- 1 tbsp. oil, or as required
- 2 lb. Boneless, skinless, chicken breasts
- Ground black pepper and salt according to taste
- 1 ½ tsp. chili powder
- ¾ cup of chicken broth
- 4 oz. cream cheese
- 2 cup of heavy whipping cream
- 1 ½ tbsp. onion powder
- 1 tsp. hot sauce
- 2 tsp. cumin
- 2 (4 oz.) cans green chilies, chopped
- 1 ½ cup of Monterey Jack cheese, grated

Instruction

- Add oil and two tbsp. Butter to a big skillet and cook over medium-high flame.
- Season the chicken with salt, black pepper, and chili powder in the meantime. Cook the chicken in skillet for five minutes, on the one hand, resisting the temptation to turn it too soon. Cook, sometimes flipping to avoid burning, until the insides are no longer pink and the juices run free, approximately ten to fifteen minutes, relying on thickness. Transfer the chicken to the plate to cool for ten minutes or before it is ready to handle. Set aside chicken that has been shredded with your fingertips.

- In a big, heavy pot, combine the remaining 6 tbsp. Butter, heavy cream, chicken broth, cream cheese, cumin, hot sauce, and onion powder. Season with the black pepper and salt, then reduce to low heat and cook for five minutes, or until the butter and cream cheese have melted.
- To the chili in a pot, add shredded chicken, Monterey Jack cheese, and green chiles. Reduce the heat to low and simmer for twenty minutes, stirring occasionally.

Keto Bread Recipes

1 Empanadas

(Ready in about 35 minutes | Serving 4 | Difficulty: Moderate)

Per serving: Kcal 554, Fat: 48g, Net Carbs: 7g, Protein: 19g

Ingredients

- 11/4 cups of almond flour
- 1/2 tsp of cream of tartar
- 1 tsp of whipping cream
- 1 tsp of baking powder
- 1 tsp of xanthan gum
- 2 tbsp of butter
- 2 eggs
- 2 tbsp of ricotta cheese

Instructions

Mix everything except half of the eggs in a bowl. Knead using the mixer's hook attachment until a ball of dough is formed. Use plastic film to wrap it and place it in the fridge for around an hour. Make squared of parchment paper. Take the dough out and dice it into pieces and make a ball out of each piece. Press every ball between 2 pieces of paper to form a flat disk. Peel the paper on the top side and use it for the rest of the balls. Split the rest of the egg into white and yolk. Whisk heavy cream and yolk. Brush balls with it and place them on a baking tray. Bake for around 20 minutes at 300 degrees F.

2 Keto bagels

(Ready in about 25 minutes | Serving 4 | Difficulty: Easy)

Per serving: Kcal 477, Fat: 39g, Net Carbs: 4g, Protein: 23g

Ingredients

Bagels

- 1 egg
- 7 oz. of mozzarella cheese
- 11/2 cups of almond flour
- 1 oz. of cream cheese
- 2 tsp of baking powder

Topping

- 1 tsp of sesame seeds
- 2 tsp of flaxseed
- 1/2 tsp of sea salt
- 1 egg
- 1/4 tsp of poppy seeds

Instructions

Preheat oven to around 430 degrees F. Line parchment paper in the baking tray. Microwave cream cheese and mozzarella in a bowl for around 1 minute. Whisk baking powder and flour in another bowl. Add egg with this mixture into cheese. Whisk to form a dough. Divide dough into 4 parts and make bun shapes. Place on a tray and form a hole in the center using the thumb. Place seasoning and seeds in a bowl and stir. Beat one more egg in a bowl and brush bagel with it. Sprinkle seasoning and bake for around 15 minutes.

3 Hot dog buns

(Ready in about 1 hour | Serving 10 | Difficulty: Hard)

Per serving: Kcal 311, Fat: 8g, Net Carbs: 1g, Protein: 4g

Ingredients

- 11/4 cups of almond flour
- 2 tsp of baking powder
- 1/3 cup of psyllium husk ground
- 1 tsp of sea salt
- 11/4 cups of boiling water
- 2 tsp of cider vinegar
- 3 eggs, only whites

Instructions

Preheat oven to around 350 degrees F. Mix dry ingredients using a bowl. Boil water and add egg whites and vinegar in a bowl and mix for around 30 seconds using a hand mixer. Make 10 pieces out of dough and roll into the shape of hot dog buns. Place in a tray and bake for around 50 minutes.

4 Cornbread

(Ready in about 25 minutes | Serving 8 | Difficulty: Easy)

Per serving: Kcal 237, Fat: 23g, Net Carbs: 1g, Protein: 7g

Ingredients

- 1/4 cup of coconut flour
- 1/3 cup of whey protein
- 1/3 cup of oat fiber
- 11/2 tsp of baking powder
- 4 oz. melted butter
- 1/4 tsp of salt
- 1/3 cup of bacon fat
- 4 eggs
- 1/4 cup of water
- 1/4 tsp corn of extract

Instructions

Preheat oven to around 350 degrees F. Oil a pan and warm in the oven. Mix dry ingredients using a bowl and add the rest of the ingredients except corn extract. Beat using a hand mixer and add corn extract. Pour mixture into the pan and bake for around 20 minutes.

5 Quick style bread

(Ready in about 15 minutes | Serving 4 | Difficulty: Easy)

Per serving: Kcal 303, Fat: 26g, Net Carbs: 5g, Protein: 10g

Ingredients

- 2 pinches of salt
- 2 oz. of cream cheese
- 2 tsp of psyllium husk ground
- 2 eggs, only whites
- 1/2 cup of almond flour
- 1/4 cup of sunflower seeds
- 1/2 cup of sesame seeds
- 11/2 tsp of baking powder

Instructions

Preheat oven to around 400 degrees F. Mix cream cheese and egg whites in a bowl. Add the rest of the ingredients and mix. Shape squares of the mixture and bake for around 12 minutes by placing them in the pan.

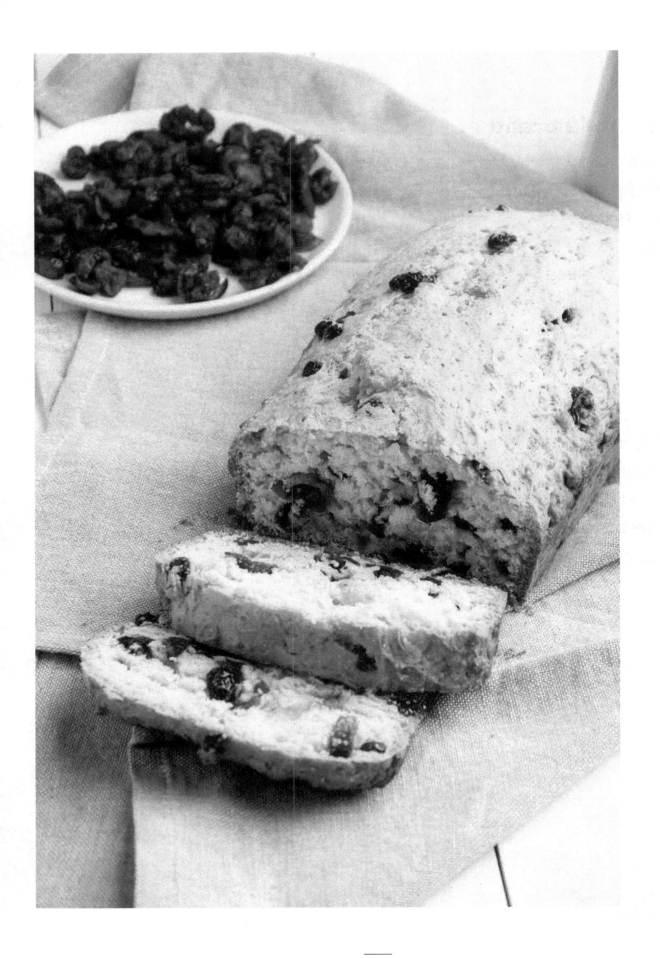

6 Mediterranean bread

(Ready in about 30 minutes | Serving 6 | Difficulty: Easy)

Per serving: Kcal 139, Fat: 12g, Net Carbs: 1g, Protein: 4g

Ingredients

- 1/2 cup of coconut flour
- 1/4 cup of olive oil
- 1/2 tbsp of black peppercorns
- 1 tbsp of psyllium husk ground
- 1 cup of boiling water
- 1/2 tsp of sea salt
- 1/2 cup of shredded parmesan
- 1/4 tsp of granulated garlic
- 1/2 tbsp of dried rosemary

Instructions

Mix dry ingredients in a bowl and add cheese and oil. Add warm water at last and stir. Line baking sheet with parchment paper and flatten dough on it. Roll out the dough to make it thin. Bake for around 25 minutes at 350 degrees F.

7 Parmesan croutons

(Ready in about 1 hour | Serving 8 | Difficulty: Hard)

Per serving: Kcal 259, Fat: 23g, Net Carbs: 1g, Protein: 8g

Ingredients

- 4 oz. of butter
- 11/4 cups of almond flour
- 3/4 cup of shredded Parmesan
- 1/3 cup of psyllium husk powder
- 1 tsp of sea salt
- 2 tsp of baking powder
- 2 tsp of cider vinegar
- 3 eggs, only whites
- 11/4 cups of boiling water

Instructions

Preheat oven to around 350 degrees F. Add dry ingredients to a bowl and mix. Boil water and add to dry ingredients with egg whites and vinegar. Beat for around 30 seconds. Form flat pieces (8) out of dough and bake for around 40 minutes in the lower rack. Split pieces of bread lengthwise and place on sheet pan face up. Stir parmesan cheese and butter and spread on bread. Broil for around 5 minutes at 450 degrees F.

8 Cloud bread

(Ready in about 30 minutes | Serving 2 | Difficulty: Easy)

Per serving: Kcal 740, Fat: 61g, Net Carbs: 7g, Protein: 37g

Ingredients

- 3 eggs
- 1 pinch of salt
- 4 oz. of cream cheese
- 1/2 tbsp of psyllium husk ground
- 1/4 tsp of cream of tartar
- 1/2 tsp of baking powder

Instructions

Preheat oven to around 300 degrees F. Add egg yolks to one bowl and whites to another. Mix salt in whites and add the rest of the ingredients to yolks. Mix two bowls and place them on a baking tray lined with paper. Spread into circles and bake for around 25 minutes.

9 Garlic focaccia

(Ready in about 25 minutes | Serving 8 | Difficulty: Easy)

Per serving: Kcal 196, Fat: 17g, Net Carbs: 2g, Protein: 8g

Ingredients

Foccacia

- 2 tbsp of cream cheese
- 11/2 cups of shredded cheese mozzarella
- 1 tsp of white wine vinegar
- 1/2 tsp of garlic powder
- 3/4 cup of almond flour
- 1 egg
- 1/2 tsp of salt

Butter

- 1/2 tsp chopped fresh rosemary
- 3 chopped garlic cloves
- 2 oz. of butter
- 1/2 tsp of sea salt

Instructions

Preheat oven to around 400 degrees F. Microwave cream cheese and mozzarella in a bowl. Add the rest of the ingredients and mix. Make the round crust by flattening the dough. Make holes and place them in a tray lined with parchment paper. Bake for around 12 minutes and mix rosemary, garlic, salt and butter in the bowl. Spread on bread and bake for another 10 minutes.

10 Parmesan chips

(Ready in about 10 minutes | Serving 2 | Difficulty: Easy)

Per serving: Kcal 263, Fat: 19g, Net Carbs: 2g, Protein: 17g

Ingredients

- 21/2 tbsp of pumpkin seeds
- 1 tbsp of chia seeds
- 3/4 cup of shredded cheese Parmesan
- 2 tbsp of whole flaxseed

Instructions

Preheat oven to around 350 degrees F. Line parchment paper on a baking sheet. Mix seeds and cheese in a bowl. Spoon mixture on a sheet in small mounds. Bake for around 10 minutes.

11 Low-carb bread

(Ready in about 30 minutes | Serving 4 | Difficulty: Easy)

Per serving: Kcal 311, Fat: 14g, Net Carbs: 2g, Protein: 6g

Ingredients

- 41/2 oz. of cream cheese
- 3 eggs
- 1 pinch of salt
- 1/2 tsp of baking powder
- 1/2 tbsp of psyllium husk ground
- 1/4 tsp of cream of tartar

Instructions

Separate whites and yolks in two bowls. Add salt to whites and mix. Mix cream cheese with yolks. Add husk powder and baking powder. Fold whites into yolk mixture. Line a baking tray with paper and add dollops of the mixture according to servings. Spread in the form of circles and bake for around 25 minutes at 300 degrees F.

12 Pizza crust

(Ready in about 35 minutes | Serving 4 | Difficulty: Moderate)

Per serving: Kcal 384, Fat: 31g, Net Carbs: 3g, Protein: 17g

Ingredients

- 11/4 cups of almond flour
- 1/4 cup of psyllium husk ground
- 1/4 cup of protein powder
- 2 tbsp of parmesan cheese grated
- 1/2 tsp of salt
- 11/2 oz. of melted butter
- 1 tbsp of Italian seasoning
- 2 eggs
- 2 tsp of baking powder
- 1 cup of boiling water
- olive oil

Instructions

Preheat oven to around 350 degrees F. Line parchment paper in two baking sheets and coat using oil. Mix dry ingredients in a bowl and stir eggs in it. Add boiling water and mix to form a thick dough. Divide in half and oil gently. Make two balls from the dough. Place on sheets and add parchment paper on the surface. Flatten balls with hands into thin crusts and discard paper. Bake for around 25 minutes. Take out and brush using coconut oil. Broil each side for around 3 minutes. Add toppings and bake for 10 more minutes at 425 degrees F.

13 Zucchini ciabatta

(Ready in about 25 minutes | Serving 4 | Difficulty: Hard)

Per serving: Kcal 409, Fat: 32g, Net Carbs: 7g, Protein: 17g

Ingredients

- 1 lb of zucchini
- 1 cup of almond flour
- sea salt
- 4 eggs
- 1/2 cup of sesame seeds
- 2 tbsp of psyllium husk ground
- 3 tbsp of sunflower seeds
- 1 tbsp of coconut flour
- 11/2 tsp of baking soda
- 1 tbsp of Italian seasoning
- 1/2 tsp of salt

Instructions

Preheat oven to around 400 degrees F. Rinse zucchini and shred finely. Squeeze extra liquid. Beat eggs in zucchini and mix dry ingredients in another bowl. Add to egg mixture and stir. Shape flat elongated pieces of bread and place on a parchment paper-lined baking sheet. Sprinkle sea salt and bake for around 20 minutes.

14 Keto dosa

(Ready in about 15 minutes | Serving 2 | Difficulty: Easy)

Per serving: Kcal 368, Fat: 33g, Net Carbs: 4g, Protein: 13g

Ingredients

- 1/2 cup of almond flour
- 1/2 tsp of coriander seed ground
- 1/2 cup of coconut milk
- 1/2 cup of shredded cheese mozzarella
- 1/2 tsp of ground cumin
- salt

Instructions

Mix everything in a bowl and warm oil in a pan. Pour batter and spread in the pan in a circular shape. Cook until cheese melts. Fold with a spatula once it is done.

15 Simple keto bread

(Ready in about 1 hour 10 minutes | Serving 6 | Difficulty: Hard)

Per serving: Kcal 311, Fat: 12g, Net Carbs: 2g, Protein: 6g

Ingredients

- 1/3 cup of psyllium husk ground
- 2 tbsp of sesame seeds
- 2 tsp of baking powder
- 11/4 cups of almond flour
- 1 tsp of sea salt
- 2 tsp of cider vinegar
- 1 cup of water
- 3 eggs, only whites

Instructions

Preheat oven to around 350 degrees F. Get a bowl to mix dry ingredients and boil water. Add egg whites and vinegar to the bowl and mix. Add boiling water and whisk into a thick dough. Make six rolls and place them on the baking sheet. Bake for around 60 minutes in the lower rack.

16 Seed crackers

(Ready in about 50 minutes | Serving 30 | Difficulty: Hard)

Per serving: Kcal 60, Fat: 6g, Net Carbs: 1g, Protein: 2g

Ingredients

- 1/3 cup of almond flour
- 1/3 cup of pumpkin seeds unsalted
- 1 tsp of salt
- 1/3 cup of flaxseed
- 1 cup of boiling water
- 1/3 cup of sesame seeds
- 1/3 cup of sunflower seeds unsalted
- 1 tbsp of psyllium husk ground
- 1/4 cup of coconut oil melted

Instructions

Preheat oven to around 300 degrees F. Add dry ingredients to a bowl and mix. Add oil and boiling water and form dough. Line parchment paper on the baking sheet and place dough. Add paper on top and flatten dough. Take the paper on top off and bake for around 45 minutes.

17 Sesame bread

(Ready in about 1 hour | Serving 30 | Difficulty: Hard)

Per serving: Kcal 61, Fat: 5g, Net Carbs: 1g, Protein: 2g

Ingredients

- 11/4 cups of sesame seeds
- 1/2 cup of cheddar cheese shredded
- 1/2 cup of sunflower seeds
- 1 tbsp of psyllium husk ground
- 2 eggs
- 1/2 cup of water
- 1/4 tsp of salt

Instructions

Preheat oven to around 350 degrees F. Line parchment paper in the baking sheet and mix everything in a bowl. Spread mixture on paper and sprinkle with salt. Bake for around 20 minutes. Take out and cut into the shape of your preference. Now bake for around 40 minutes at 275 degrees F.

18 Holiday bread

(Ready in about 1 hour | Serving 22 | Difficulty: Hard)

Per serving: Kcal 151, Fat: 12g, Net Carbs: 2g, Protein: 5g

Ingredients

- 2 cups of almond flour
- 1/3 cup of sesame seeds
- 1/2 cup of coconut flour
- 1 cup of sour cream
- 1/3 cup of flaxseed
- 1 tbsp of baking powder
- 1/4 cup of psyllium husk ground
- 3/4 tbsp of ground cloves
- 1/2 tbsp of fennel seeds
- 1/2 tbsp of orange peel ground
- 1 tsp of anise seeds
- 1 tsp of salt
- 1 tsp of ground cardamom
- 6 eggs
- 3 oz. of cream cheese

Instructions

Preheat the oven to 400 degrees F. Add dry ingredients to a bowl and mix. Mix cream cheese, eggs and sour cream in another bowl. Add to dry mixture and stir. Line a pan with parchment paper and pour the mixture on it. Bake for around 60 minutes.

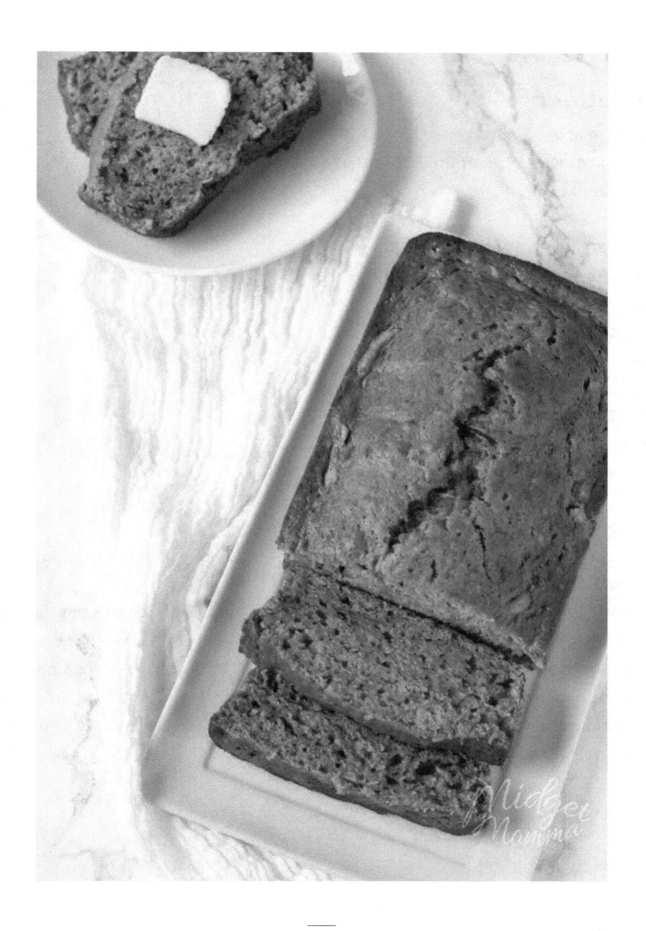

19 Butter bread

(Ready in about 1 hour | Serving 20 | Difficulty: Hard)

Per serving: Kcal 91, Fat: 8g, Net Carbs: 1g, Protein: 2g

Ingredients

Bread

- 11/4 cups of almond flour
- 5 tbsp of psyllium husk ground
- 2 tsp of baking powder
- 1 tsp of sea salt
- 1 cup of water
- 2 tsp of cider vinegar
- 3 eggs, only whites

Garlic butter

- 4 oz. of butter
- 1 minced garlic clove
- 2 tbsp chopped fresh parsley
- 1/2 tsp of salt

Instructions

Preheat oven to around 350 degrees F. Line parchment paper on the baking sheet and mix dry ingredients in a bowl. Boil water and add egg whites, vinegar and water to dry ingredients. Whisk for around 30 seconds. Roll into hot dog-shaped buns and place them on a sheet. Bake for around 40 minutes. Mix ingredients for garlic butter and refrigerate. Cut buns from the center and spread butter. Bake for 15 minutes at 425 degrees F.

20 Bread twists

(Ready in about 25 minutes | Serving 10 | Difficulty: Easy)

Per serving: Kcal 181, Fat: 16g, Net Carbs: 1g, Protein: 7g

Ingredients

- 1/2 cup of almond flour
- 1/2 tsp of salt
- 1/4 cup of green pesto
- 1/4 cup of coconut flour
- 1 tsp of baking powder
- 2 oz. of butter
- 1 beaten egg
- 12/3 cups of shredded cheese mozzarella
- 1 beaten egg

Instructions

Preheat oven to around 350 degrees F. Add dry ingredients to a bowl and mix. Whisk eggs in a mixture and use a pot to melt cheese and butter. Add to bowl and make a firm dough by mixing. Place parchment paper and add dough to it. Form a rectangle with a rolling pin. Add pesto over dough and dice into strips(1 inch approx.). Twist and place on a parchment paper-lined baking sheet. Bake for around 20 minutes.

21 French toast

(Ready in about 10 minutes | Serving 2 | Difficulty: Easy)

Per serving: Kcal 408, Fat: 37g, Net Carbs: 3g, Protein: 15g

Ingredients

Bread

- 2 tbsp of almond flour
- 2 tbsp of whipping cream
- 1 tsp of butter
- 2 tbsp of coconut flour
- 1 pinch of salt
- 11/2 tsp of baking powder
- 2 eggs

Batter

- 1 pinch of salt
- 2 tbsp of whipping cream
- 2 eggs
- 1/2 tsp of ground cinnamon
- 2 tbsp of butter

Instructions

Coat a glass dish with butter. Mix dry ingredients and break an egg. Stir and microwave for around 2 minutes. Take out of dish and dice in two pieces. Mix the rest of the ingredients in a bowl and pour on slices. Fry in butter and enjoy.

22 Soft tortillas

(Ready in about 20 minutes | Serving 6 | Difficulty: Easy)

Per serving: Kcal 236, Fat: 21g, Net Carbs: 1g, Protein: 5g

Ingredients

- 1/4 tsp of baking soda
- 11/2 cups of hot water
- 1 cup of coconut flour
- 1/2 tsp of salt
- 1/2 cup of avocado oil
- 1/4 cup of psyllium husk ground
- 3 egg whites

Instructions

Warm oil in a pan and mix baking soda, salt and coconut flour in a bowl. Whisk husk and drizzle oil. Fold in whites and add hot water, around 1/2 cup at once. Combine to form dough and shape into 12 balls. Place balls between parchment and flatten using a tortilla press. Toast each side for around 3 minutes.

23 Nut-free bread

(Ready in about 40 minutes | Serving 20 | Difficulty: Moderate)

Per serving: Kcal 109, Fat: 9g, Net Carbs: 1g, Protein: 6g

Ingredients

- 1 tbsp melted butter
- 6 eggs
- 1 oz. of cream cheese
- 3 cups of shredded cheese
- 2 tbsp of psyllium husk ground
- 1/2 cup of oat fiber
- 3 tsp of baking powder
- 1/2 tsp of salt

Topping

- 2 tbsp of poppy seeds
- 3 tbsp of sesame seeds

Instructions

Preheat oven to around 360 degrees F. Whisk eggs and add rest of ingredients in a bowl except butter. Coat a pan using butter and spread dough using a spatula. Sprinkle seeds on the dough and bake for around 35 minutes.

24 Fluffy bread

(Ready in about 1 hour 20 minutes | Serving 18 | Difficulty: Hard)

Per serving: Kcal 82, Fat: 7g, Net Carbs: 3g, Protein: 4g

Ingredients

- 1 cup of Almond Flour
- 1/3 cup of Butter
- 2 tsp of baking powder Gluten-free
- 1/4 cup of Coconut Flour
- 1/4 tsp of Sea salt
- 12 Egg whites

Instructions

Preheat oven to around 325 degrees F. Line parchment paper on a pan and add all the ingredients except tartar and eggs to the processor. Pulse and beat egg whites and tartar in a bowl using a hand mixer. Add half amount of whites to the processor and pulse. Transfer to bowl with rest of whites. Fold gently and place in pan. Bake for around 40 minutes. Bake for another 30 minutes after covering with foil.

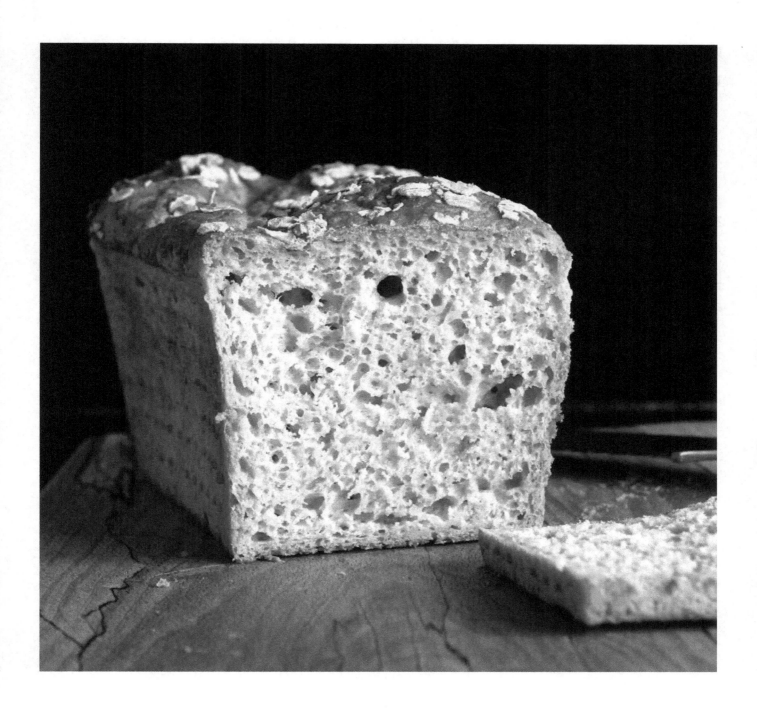

25 90 Seconds Bread

(Ready in about 2 minutes | Serving 1 | Difficulty: Easy)

Per serving: Kcal 220, Fat: 21g, Net Carbs: 4g, Protein: 4g

Ingredients

- 1 tbsp of coconut flour
- 1 egg
- 1 tbsp of butter
- 1/2 tsp of baking powder double acting

Instructions

Add butter to a bowl and microwave. Mix the rest of the ingredients in butter and beat. Microwave for around 2 minutes and slice in two parts. Preheat oven to around 375 degrees F and bake for around 12 minutes.

26 Almond Flour Bread

(Ready in about 50 minutes | Serving 12 | Difficulty: Hard)

Per serving: Kcal 156, Fat: 14.2g, Net Carbs: 3.6g, Protein: 5.2g

Ingredients

- 2 whites of eggs
- pinch of salt
- 2 cups almond flour
- 2 eggs, yolks & whites
- 1/4 cup of butter melted
- 1 1/2 tsp of baking powder
- 4 tbsp of psyllium husks
- 1/2 tsp of xanthan gum
- 1/2 cup of warm water

Instructions

Preheat oven to around 350 degrees F. Break 2 eggs and 2 whites and beat. Add the rest of the ingredients and make a smooth dough by blending. Fill the baking tin and bake for around 45 minutes.

27 Plain Bread

(Ready in about 1 hour | Serving 12 | Difficulty: Hard)

Per serving: Kcal 247, Fat: 22.8g, Net Carbs: 4.9g, Protein: 7.7g

Ingredients

- 7 eggs
- cooking spray
- 1/2tsp of xanthan gum
- 1/2 cup melted butter
- 2 cups of almond flour blanched
- 2 tbsp of olive oil
- 1 tsp of baking powder
- 1/2tsp of sea salt

Instructions

Preheat oven to around 350 degrees F. Coat a pan using cooking spray and break and beat eggs in a bowl. Add butter and oil and mix. Mix the rest of the ingredients in another bowl. Add to eggs and mix. Pour in pan and bake for around 45 minutes.

28 Fathead Bread

(Ready in about 55 minutes | Serving 4 | Difficulty: Hard)

Per serving: Kcal 240, Fat: 19.4g, Net Carbs: 4.2g, Protein: 13.5g

Ingredients

- 3/4 cup of shredded cheese mozzarella
- 1 egg
- 2 ounces of cream cheese
- 1/3 cup of almond flour
- 1/4tsp of garlic powder
- 2 tsp of baking powder
- 1/2 cup of shredded cheese Cheddar

Instructions

Microwave cream cheese and mozzarella in a bowl for around 20 seconds. Beat eggs in a bowl and add the rest of the ingredients. Add mozzarella mixture and mix. Transfer to plastic wrap and wrap over dough. Form a ball and place it in the fridge for around 30 minutes. Preheat oven to around 425 degrees F and oil a parchment paper-lined baking sheet. Take the dough out and remove the wrap. Make 4 pieces and roll each into the shape of a ball. Cut in half and place on sheet. Bake for around 12 minutes.

29 Bread Rolls

(Ready in about 1 hour 5 minutes | Serving 8 | Difficulty: Hard)

Per serving: Kcal 166, Fat: 12g, Net Carbs: 10g, Protein: 6.8g

Ingredients

- cooking spray
- 5 tbsp of psyllium husk
- 2 tbsp of sesame seeds
- 1 1/2 cups of almond flour blanched
- 1 tsp of sea salt
- 3 eggs, only whites
- 1 cup of boiling water
- 2 tsp of white vinegar

Instructions

Preheat oven to around 350 degrees F. Oil a baking sheet using cooking spray. Add the rest of the ingredients to a bowl and mix using an electric mixer to form a dough. Make 8 rolls from the dough and place them on a sheet. Sprinkle seeds and bake for around 55 minutes.

30 Simple and Easy Bread

(Ready in about 1 hour 10 minutes | Serving 1 | Difficulty: Hard)

Per serving: Kcal 450, Fat: 40g, Net Carbs: 10g, Protein: 19g

Ingredients

- 6 eggs
- 1 tbsp of baking powder
- 1/4 cup of melted butter
- 1/2 tsp of cream of tartar
- 1 1/2 cup of finely ground almond flour
- 1/2 tsp of kosher salt

Instructions

Preheat oven to around 375 degrees F. Line parchment paper in a pan and separate egg yolks and whites. Combine whites with tartar in a bowl and beat yolk with the rest of the ingredients in another bowl. Fold in whites and transfer to pan. Bake for around 30 minutes.

31 Gluten-free Bread

(Ready in about 1 hour 15 minutes | Serving 10 | Difficulty: Hard)

Per serving: Kcal 53, Fat: 3g, Net Carbs: 4g, Protein: 2g

Ingredients

- 1 1/4 cups of almond flour
- 2 tbsp of sesame seeds
- 2 tsp of baking powder
- 5 tbsp of psyllium husk ground
- 1 tsp of salt
- 1 cup of boiling water
- 2 tsp of apple cider vinegar
- 3 eggs, only whites

Instructions

Preheat oven to around 350 degrees F. Line parchment paper in loaf tin after coating with butter. Combine husk, salt, almond flour and baking powder in a bowl. Add cider vinegar and egg whites to dry ingredients and mix using an electric mixer. Add boiling water slowly and mix. A dough will form. Transfer to the tin and sprinkle seeds. Bake for around 60 minutes.

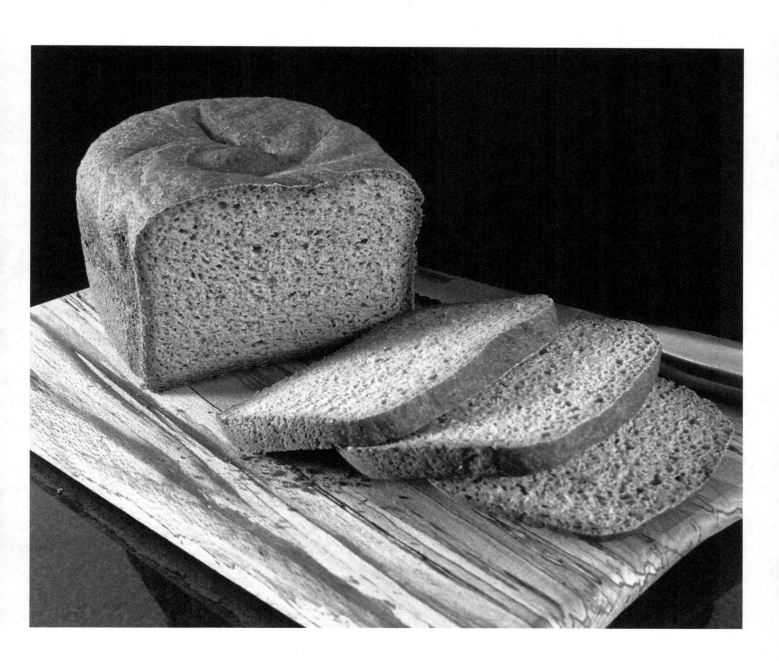

32 Collagen Bread

(Ready in about 1 hour 50 minutes | Serving 12 | Difficulty: Hard)

Per serving: Kcal 311, Fat: 5g, Net Carbs: 1g, Protein: 7g

Ingredients

- 1/2 cup of Collagen Protein Grass-Fed
- 1 tsp of xanthan gum
- 6 tbsp of almond flour
- 5 separated eggs, pastured
- 1 tbsp of coconut oil unflavored
- 1 tsp of baking powder aluminum-free
- Pinch of Himalayan salt

Instructions

Preheat oven to around 325 degrees F. Oil a loaf dish and beat egg whites in a bowl. Mix dry ingredients in another bowl. Mix yolks, coconut oil and wet ingredients in another bowl. Add both mixtures to whites and beat. Pour into the dish and bake for around 40 minutes.

33 Coconut Bread

(Ready in about 1 hour 10 minutes | Serving 10 | Difficulty: Hard)

Per serving: Kcal 318, Fat: 17g, Net Carbs: 9g, Protein: 12g

Ingredients

- 1/2 cup coconut flour
- 1/4 cup of coconut oil
- 1/4 tsp of baking soda
- 1/4 tsp of salt
- 6 eggs
- 1/4 of almond milk unsweetened

Instructions

Preheat your oven to around 350 degrees F. Line parchment paper in a pan and combine salt, soda and coconut flour in a bowl. Mix oil, milk and eggs in another bowl. Incorporate both mixtures and pour in pan. Bake for around 50 minutes.

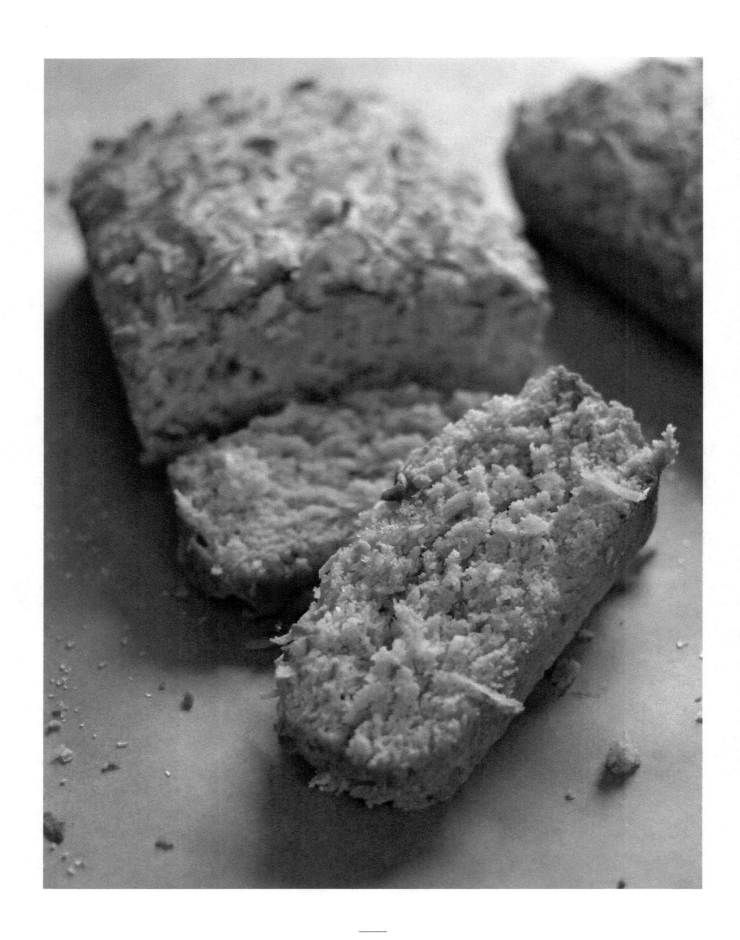

34 Macadamia Bread

(Ready in about 35 minutes | Serving 10 | Difficulty: Moderate)

Per serving: Kcal 151, Fat: 14g, Net Carbs: 4g, Protein: 5g

Ingredients

- 5 oz of macadamia nuts
- 1/2 tsp of apple cider vinegar
- 1/4 cup of coconut flour
- 5 eggs
- 1/2 tsp of baking soda

Instructions

Preheat oven to around 350 degrees F. Pulse nuts in processor and add eggs, and pulse again. Add rest of ingredients and pulse to incorporate thoroughly. Oil a pan and pour the mixture, and bake for around 40 minutes.

35 Cauliflower Bread

(Ready in about 1 hour 18 minutes | Serving 6 | Difficulty: Hard)

Per serving: Kcal 108, Fat: 8g, Net Carbs: 8g, Protein: 6g

Ingredients

- 3 cups of riced cauliflower
- 1 tbsp chopped fresh rosemary
- 1 1/4 cup of Coconut Flour Wholesome
- 10 separated Egg
- 1 1/2 tbsp of baking powder Gluten-free
- 1 tbsp chopped fresh parsley

Instructions

Preheat oven to around 350 degrees F. Line parchment paper in a pan and steam cauliflower in the microwave until it is soft. Beat egg whites and tartar in a bowl with a mixer. Add the rest of the ingredients with a quarter of whites in the processor. Squeeze cauliflower in a kitchen towel to dry it. Add to blender and pulse. Add rest of whites and pulse. Fold in the rosemary and parsley. Transfer to pan and bake for around 50 minutes.

36 Tortillas

(Ready in about 15 minutes | Serving 8 | Difficulty: Easy)

Per serving: Kcal 89, Fat: 6g, Net Carbs: 4g, Protein: 3g

Ingredients

- 96 g of almond flour
- 3 tsp of water
- 2 tsp of xanthan gum
- 24 g of coconut flour
- 1 tsp of baking powder
- 2 tsp of apple cider vinegar
- 1/4 tsp of kosher salt
- 1 beaten egg

Instructions

Break eggs in a bowl and whisk. Add rest of ingredients except cider vinegar in processor and blend. Add cider vinegar while the blender is running. Once it is uniformly distributed, add eggs and water. Once a ball forms from the dough, stop. Wrap using cling film and through plastic, knead for around 1 minute. Warm a pan and form eight balls of 1 inch. Roll out balls in two parchment papers. Place in pan and cook for around 6 seconds. Flip and cook until each side is a bit golden.

37 Buttery Flatbread

(Ready in about 7 minutes | Serving 2 | Difficulty: Easy)

Per serving: Kcal 232, Fat: 19g, Net Carbs: 9g, Protein: 9g

Ingredients

- 1 cup of Almond Flour
- 1 tbsp of Oil
- 2 tsp of Xanthan Gum
- 2 tbsp of Coconut Flour
- 1/2 tsp of Baking Powder
- 1 Egg plus 1 Egg White
- 1/2 tsp of Falk Salt
- 1 tbsp of Water
- 1 tbsp of melted Butter

Instructions

Mix dry ingredients in a bowl. Add eggs to flour and mix. Add water and work with dough, so moisture is absorbed. Make 4 parts of dough and press using cling wrap. Warm oil in the pan and fry each side of bread for around 1 minute. Brush butter on top and garnish using parsley and salt.

38 Gluten-Free Biscuits

(Ready in about 30 minutes | Serving 6 | Difficulty: Easy)

Per serving: Kcal 290, Fat: 30g, Net Carbs: 8g, Protein: 7g

Ingredients

- 1 egg
- 2 tsp. of apple vinegar
- 77 g of sour cream
- 2 tbsp of water
- 96 g of almond flour
- 1 tbsp of apple cider vinegar
- 63 g of flaxseed meal golden
- 20 g of whey protein
- 21 g of coconut flour
- 3 1/2 tsp of baking powder
- 1/2 tsp of kosher salt
- 1 tsp of xanthan gum
- 112 g of organic butter grass-fed

Instructions

Preheat your oven to around 450 degrees F. Line parchment paper in a tray. Mix eggs, water, apple vinegar and sour cream in a bowl. Add rest of ingredients except butter in blender and pulse. Add butter and blend again. Pour bowl mixture and blend until incorporated. Make 6 rounds from dough and place in the tray. Brush butter and place in oven. Bake for around 20 minutes.

39 Cauliflower Buns

(Ready in about 45 minutes | Serving 6 | Difficulty: Hard)

Per serving: Kcal 43, Fat: 1.9g, Net Carbs: 3.5g, Protein: 3.3g

Ingredients

- 2 cups of cauliflower rice
- 2 tbsp of coconut flour
- 2 beaten eggs
- 1/4 tsp of ground turmeric
- 1/4 tsp of black pepper ground
- 1/2 tsp of sea salt

Instructions

Preheat your oven to around 400 degrees F. Line parchment paper on the baking sheet. Mix everything in a bowl and make six buns from the batter. Place on sheet and bake for around 30 minutes.

40 Low Carb Biscuits

(Ready in about 25 minutes | Serving 12 | Difficulty: Easy)

Per serving: Kcal 164, Fat: 15g, Net Carbs: 4g, Protein: 5g

Ingredients

- 1/3 cup of Butter
- 2 cups of Blanched Wholesome Yum Almond Flour
- 1/2 tsp of Sea salt
- 2 tsp of baking powder Gluten-free
- 2 whisked egg

Instructions

Preheat oven to around 350 degrees F. Line parchment paper on the baking sheet. Add all the ingredients to a bowl and whisk. Scoop on the sheet in the amount of tbsp. Form biscuit shapes and bake for around 15 minutes.

41 Pizza Crust

(Ready in about 10 minutes | Serving 4| Difficulty: Easy)

Per serving: Kcal 125, Fat: 10g, Net Carbs: 6g, Protein: 8g

Ingredients

- 1 tbsp of coconut flour
- 8 egg whites
- 1/2 tsp of baking powder
- 1/4 cup of sifted coconut flour
- Pepper, salt and Italian spices

Pizza sauce

- 1 tsp of dried basil
- 2 cloves of garlic crushed
- 1/2 cup of tomato sauce
- 1/4 tsp of sea salt

Instructions

Whisk egg in a bowl and add coconut flour. Whisk and add mixed spices and baking powder and keep whisking until fully incorporated. Warm a pan after oiling it lightly. Pour mixture into the pan and cook for around 4 minutes. Flip and cook for 2 more minutes. Dust with coconut flour. Combine sauce ingredients in a bowl and spread on crust.

42 Zucchini Bread

(Ready in about 1 hour 20 minutes | Serving 16 | Difficulty: Hard)

Per serving: Kcal 200, Fat: 17g, Net Carbs: 2.6g, Protein: 6g

Ingredients

- 3 eggs
- 1 tsp of vanilla extract
- 1/2cup of olive oil
- 2 1/2cups of almond flour
- 1 cup of grated zucchini
- 1/2tsp of salt
- 1 1/2 cups of erythritol
- 1 1/2tsp of baking powder
- 1 tsp of ground cinnamon
- 1/2tsp of nutmeg
- 1/4tsp of ground ginger
- 1/2cup of chopped walnuts

Instructions

Preheat your oven to around 350 degrees F. Mix oil, eggs and vanilla in a bowl. Mix erythritol, baking powder, salt, nutmeg, almond flour, ginger and cinnamon in another bowl. Squeeze zucchini in a paper towel and add to eggs. Add dry ingredients to the egg and blend. Spray a pan using cooking spray and spoon mixture. Add walnuts and press with a spatula. Bake for around 70 minutes.

43 Blueberry Muffin Bread

(Ready in about 1 hour | Serving 12 | Difficulty: Hard)

Per serving: Kcal 156, Fat: 13g, Net Carbs: 4g, Protein: 5g

Ingredients

- 1/4 cup of butter
- 1/2 cup of almond butter
- 5 eggs
- 1/2 cup of almond flour
- 2 tsp of baking powder
- 1/2 tsp of salt
- 1/2 cup of almond milk
- 1/2 cup of blueberries

Instructions

Preheat the oven to around 350 degrees F. Melt butter and nut butter in a bowl and stir. Mix baking powder, salt and almond flour in another bowl and pour butter mixture. Stir and take another bowl to mix eggs and almond milk. Pour in flour and butter mixture and stir. Add blueberries and stir. Line parchment paper in the pan and oil it. Pour batter and bake for around 45 minutes.

44 Cranberry Bread

(Ready in about 1 hour 25 minutes | Serving 12 | Difficulty: Hard)

Per serving: Kcal 175, Fat: 14g, Net Carbs: 8g, Protein: 7g

Ingredients

- 1 1/2 cups of almond flour
- 1/2 cup of white sweetener
- 1/2 cup of almond milk unsweetened
- 1/2 cup of coconut flour
- 1/2tsp of 30% extract monk fruit
- 1 1/2tsp of baking powder
- 1 tbsp of orange peel dried
- 1/2tsp of baking soda
- 1/2tsp of ground cinnamon
- 1/2tsp of xanthan gum
- 1/2tsp of salt
- 1/4 cup of butter melted unsalted
- 1/4tsp of ground nutmeg
- 6 eggs
- 6 ounces of cranberries

Instructions

Preheat oven to around 325 degrees F. Oil a pan and line using parchment paper. Mix everything except butter, egg and almond milk in a bowl. Mix them in a separate bowl. Add to dry ingredients and whisk. Fold the mixture in cranberries and pour in a pan. Bake for around 1 hour.

45 Fluffy Buns

(Ready in about 30 minutes | Serving 4 | Difficulty: Easy)

Per serving: Kcal 109, Fat: 12.5g, Net Carbs: 2.3g, Protein: 7.3g

Ingredients

- 1 egg
- 1 tsp of baking powder
- 3 eggs, only whites
- 1/4 cup of hot water
- 1/4 cup of coconut flour
- 1/4 cup of almond flour
- 1 tbsp of psyllium husk ground
- Sesame seeds

Instructions

Preheat oven to around 356 F and mix dry ingredients in a bowl. Add everything to the blender and blend for around 20 seconds. Make four portions from dough and shape buns. Place on sheet and sprinkle seeds on top. Bake for around 25 minutes.

46 Ultimate Buns

(Ready in about 1 hour | Serving 1 | Difficulty: Hard)

Per serving: Kcal 208, Fat: 15.2g, Net Carbs: 4.2g, Protein: 10.1g

Dry ingredients

- 2/3 cup of psyllium husks ground
- 1 1/2 cup of almond flour
- 1/2 cup of coconut flour
- 5 tbsp of sesame seeds2 tsp of garlic powder
- 1/2 cup of flax meal
- 2 tsp of onion powder
- 1 tsp of baking soda
- 2 tsp of cream of tartar
- 1 tsp of Himalayan salt

Wet ingredients
- 2 eggs
- 6 egg whites
- 2 cups of water

Instructions

Preheat oven to around 350 degrees F. Add dry ingredients except for sesame seeds and mix. Add eggs and mix. Make buns with a spoon. Line a tray using parchment paper and place buns. Top with seeds and bake for around 55 minutes.

47 Dinner Rolls

(Ready in about 15 minutes | Serving 6 | Difficulty: Easy)

Per serving: Kcal 219, Fat: 18g, Net Carbs: 5.6g, Protein: 16g10.7g

Ingredients

- 1 Cup of Mozzarella, shredded
- 1 Cup of Almond Flour
- 1 oz of Cream Cheese
- 1/4 Cup of Flax Seed Ground
- 1/2 Tsp of Baking Soda
- 1 egg

Instructions

Preheat the oven to around 400 degrees F. Line parchment paper on the baking sheet. Microwave mozzarella and cream cheese in a bowl. Stir and add eggs. Combine baking soda, flax and almond flour in another bowl. Add egg mixture and cheese to this mixture. Make 6 balls from the dough. Place on sheet and bake for around 12 minutes.

48 Bagel Scones

(Ready in about 40 minutes | Serving 12 | Difficulty: Moderate)

Per serving: Kcal 161, Fat: 13.5g, Net Carbs: 6.5g, Protein: 5.7g

Ingredients

- 2 cups of almond flour
- 1 tbsp of baking powder
- 1/4 cup of coconut flour
- 1/2 tsp of garlic powder
- 2 eggs
- 1/4 tsp of salt
- 1/4 cup of whipping cream
- 2 tbsp of Bagel Seasoning
- 1 tbsp of butter melted

Instructions

Preheat the oven to around 325 degrees F. Line parchment paper on the baking sheet and oil it gently. Mix everything except bagel seasoning, whipping cream and egg in a bowl. Then stir whipping cream and egg until you get a dough. Place on sheet and shape into a rectangle roughly. Make 6 squares with a knife and cut diagonally each to make two triangles. Sprinkle with bagel seasoning and bake for around 25 minutes.

49 Avocado bread

(Ready in about 1 hour 35 minutes | Serving 9 | Difficulty: Hard)

Per serving: Kcal 214, Fat: 19.1g, Net Carbs: 4.5g, Protein: 10.3g

Ingredients

- 1 cup of almond flour
- 2 tbsp of Swerve Sweetener
- 1/3 cup of whey protein
- 2 tsp of baking powder
- 3 eggs, separated
- 1/2 tsp of salt
- 1 large egg
- 2 tbsp of water
- 3 tbsp of avocado oil
- 1/2 tsp of cream of tartar

Instructions

Preheat oven to around 325 degrees F and line parchment paper in the pan. Mix dry ingredients in one bowl and wet ingredients except tartar and whites in a separate bowl. Add egg mixture to dry ingredients and whisk to combine. Beat whites and tartar in another bowl and fold whites in the batter. Pour batter into the pan and cook for around 50 minutes.

50 Croissants

(Ready in about 50 minutes | Serving 8 | Difficulty: Hard)

Per serving: Kcal 141, Fat: 9.6g, Net Carbs: 4.6g, Protein: 8.4g

Ingredients

- 1 tbsp melted butter
- 1/4 cup of coconut flour
- 1/2 tsp of xanthan gum
- 2 tbsp of Sweetener
- 1 tsp of baking powder
- 1 egg
- 6 ounces of mozzarella
- 1/3 tbsp of almond paste
- 1 tbsp of sliced almonds

Instructions

Preheat oven to around 400 degrees F. Line a baking sheet and whisk coconut flour, xantham gum, baking powder and sweetener in a bowl. Melt cheese in the microwave for around 30 seconds. Knead after stirring in the egg and flour mixture in the bowl with a spatula. Pour on the sheet and cover with parchment paper. Roll into a circle of 12 inches. Take 1.5 tbsp of almond paste and shape a thin log of length around 3 inches. Position at the wide end of 1 wedge and fold the dough around almond paste tightly. Pinch to seal and repeat with the rest of the dough. Curve ends of dough to make a crescent shape. Add sliced almonds and bake for around 25 minutes after turning the temperature to 350 degrees F. Dust using sweetener.

51 Gluten-Free Bagels

(Ready in about 30 minutes | Serving 6 | Difficulty: Easy)

Per serving: Kcal 364, Fat: 27.9g, Sodium 919.8mg, Protein: 20.9g

Ingredients

- 1 tbsp. baking powder, gluten-free
- 1 ½ cups of almond flour
- 2 eggs
- 1 tsp. garlic salt
- 2 oz. cream cheese, cubed
- 2 ½ cups of shredded mozzarella cheese

Instructions

- Preheat oven to 400 degrees Fahrenheit. Using parchment paper, line the baking sheet.
- In a mixing bowl, add the baking powder, garlic salt, and almond flour.
- In the microwave-safe bowl, mix mozzarella and cream cheese. Microwave for one minute, then remove and mix. Microwave for another minute, then take it off and stir until all is well combined. Working fast, stir the eggs and flour mixture into melted cheese mixture. Knead the dough by hand until it becomes a sticky dough. Continue kneading and pressing the dough for approximately two minutes or until it is fully uniform.
- The dough can be divided into six equal bits. Roll each one into the long log, then push the ends together to form a bagel shape and put it on the baking sheet that has been prepared.
- For ten to fourteen minutes in the preheated oven, bake till the bagels are golden.

52 Fluffy Keto Pancakes

(Ready in about 10 minutes | Serving 4 | Difficulty: Easy)

Per serving: Kcal 383, Fat: 32.2g, Sodium 842.3mg, Protein: 15.3g

Ingredients

- ¼ cup of coconut flour
- 1 cup of almond flour
- 2 tbsp. natural sweetener, low-calorie
- 1 tsp. baking powder
- 1 tsp. salt
- ½ tsp. ground cinnamon
- ¼ cup of heavy whipping cream, at room temp.
- 6 eggs, at room temp.
- 1 tsp. vanilla extract
- 2 tbsp. melted butter

Directions

- In a mixing bowl, add coconut flour, almond flour, salt, sweetener, cinnamon, and baking powder. Slowly whisk in the heavy cream, eggs, vanilla extract, and butter till just mixed.
- Over medium-high flame, gently oil a griddle. Cook till the bubbles form and the sides are dry, three to four minutes, by dropping batter by big spoonfuls onto griddle. Cook for two or three minutes on the other hand, until browned. Continue with the remaining batter.
- Cholesterol 281.2mg

53 High Protein Bread

(Ready in about 2hrs 40 mins | Serving 10 | Difficulty: Medium)

Per serving: Kcal 137, Fat: 2.4g, Sodium 235mg, Protein: 6.5g

Ingredients

- 2 tsp dry yeast active
- 1 cup of bread flour
- 1 cup of flour whole wheat
- ¼ cup of soy flour
- ¼ cup of soymilk powder
- ¼ cup of oat bran
- 1 tbsp of canola oil
- 1 tbsp of honey
- 1 tsp of salt
- 1 cup of water

Directions

In the bread machine pan, arrange the ingredients in an order prescribed by the maker. Choose between the standard medium and regular settings; click Start.

Keto Chaffle Recipes

1 Oreo Chaffles

(Ready in about 23 minutes | Serving 2 | Difficulty: Easy)

Per serving: Kcal 1381, Fat: 146g, Net Carbs: 14g, Protein: 17g

Ingredients

- 1/2 cup of Sugar-Free Chocolate Chips
- 1 tsp of Vanilla extract
- 3 Eggs
- 1/2 cup of butter
- 1/4 cup of sweetener

Cheese Frosting

- 4 ounces of Cream Cheese
- 4 ounces of butter
- 1/2 cup of Powdered Swerve
- 1 tsp of Vanilla extract
- 1/4 cup of Whipping Cream

Instructions

Melt chocolate and butter in a bowl in the microwave for around 1 minute. Stir to remove clumps. Mix vanilla, egg and sweetener in a bowl. Pour a quarter of the mixture into the waffle maker and cook for around 8 minutes. Mix frosting ingredients in the food processor's bowl in the meantime and make a smooth mixture. Spread frosting among two chaffles.

2 Strawberry Chaffles

(Ready in about 35 minutes | Serving 8 | Difficulty: Moderate)

Per serving: Kcal 189, Fat: 14.3g, Net Carbs: 5.2g, Protein: 10g

Ingredients

- 3 oz of cream cheese
- 1 cup of whipped cream
- 2 beaten eggs
- 2 cups shredded mozzarella cheese
- 1/2 cup of almond flour
- 2 tsp of baking powder
- 3 tbsp of sweetener
- 8 strawberries
- 1 tbsp of sweetener

Instructions

Add mozzarella and cream cheese to a bowl and microwave for around 1 minute. Beat eggs and mix with baking powder, 3 tbsp sweetener and almond flour. Mix it with cheese and add to 2 diced strawberries. Place in the fridge for around 20 minutes. Dice the rest of the strawberries and add tbsp sweetener. Warm waffle iron and add the quarter mixture from the fridge to the center of the iron. Cook for around 7 minutes.

3 Chocolate Chaffle

(Ready in about 18 minutes | Serving 2 | Difficulty: Easy)

Per serving: Kcal 672, Fat: 70g, Net Carbs: 11g, Protein: 13g

Ingredients

- 1/2 cup of Chocolate Chips
- 1/4 cup of sweetener
- 3 Eggs
- 1/2 cup of butter
- 1 tsp of Vanilla extract

Instructions

Melt chocolate and butter in a bowl in the microwave for around 1 minute. Stir and remove clumps. Blend sweetener, vanilla and eggs in a bowl. Add chocolate and butter and whisk. Pour the quarter amount of mixture into a waffle maker. Cook for around 8 minutes.

4 Pumpkin Chaffles

(Ready in about 7 minutes | Serving 1 | Difficulty: Easy)

Per serving: Kcal 250, Fat: 15g, Net Carbs: 5g, Protein: 23g

Ingredients

- 1/2 cup mozzarella cheese shredded
- 1 1/2tbsp of pumpkin purée
- 1 beaten egg
- 1/2tsp of Swerve confectioners
- 1/4tsp of Pumpkin Pie Spice
- 1/2tsp of vanilla extract
- ⅛ tsp of maple extract

Instructions

Mix all the ingredients except mozzarella cheese in a bowl and mix. Add cheese and whisk. Spray waffle using cooking spray. Place half amount of batter in the center of the waffle maker. Cook for around 6 minutes. Repeat with the remaining batter.

5 Basic Chaffle

(Ready in about 8 minutes | Serving 2 | Difficulty: Easy)

Per serving: Kcal 208, Fat: 16g, Net Carbs: 4g, Protein: 11g

Ingredients

- 1 Big Egg
- 2 tbsp of Almond Flour
- 1/2 cup shredded Mozzarella cheese

Instructions

Preheat waffle iron for around 5 minutes. Microwave cheese for around 30 seconds. Add the rest of the ingredients and mix. Pour mixture that covers the surface of the waffle maker. Cook for around 4 minutes. Take out and place on a plate and repeat with the rest of the batter.

6 Garlic Chaffles

(Ready in about 8 minutes | Serving 2 | Difficulty: Easy)

Per serving: Kcal 208, Fat: 16g, Net Carbs: 4g, Protein: 11g

Ingredients

- 1/3 cup Parmesan cheese Grated
- 1/2 cup shredded Mozzarella cheese
- 1 Big Egg
- 1/2 tsp of Italian seasoning
- 1 minced Garlic clove

Instructions

Preheat waffle iron for around 5 minutes. Microwave cream cheese for around 30 seconds. Add the rest of the ingredients except the toppings. Pour mixture that covers the surface of the waffle maker. Cook for around 4 minutes. Take out and place on a plate and repeat with the rest of the batter.

7 Cinnamon Chaffles

(Ready in about 8 minutes | Serving 2 | Difficulty: Easy)

Per serving: Kcal 208, Fat: 16g, Net Carbs: 4g, Protein: 11g

Ingredients

- 3/4 cup shredded Mozzarella cheese
- 1 Big Egg
- 2 tbsp of Almond Flour
- 2 tbsp of besti erythritol
- 1/2 tbsp melted butter
- 1/2 tsp of cinnamon
- 1 tbsp melted butter
- 1/2 tsp of vanilla extract
- 3/4 tsp of cinnamon
- 1/4 cup of besti erythritol

Instructions

Preheat waffle iron for around 5 minutes. Microwave cream cheese for around 30 seconds. Add the rest of the ingredients except the toppings. Pour mixture that covers the surface of the waffle maker. Cook for around 4 minutes. Take out and place on a plate and repeat with the rest of the batter. To prepare churro chaffles, mix cinnamon and erythritol for topping. Brush chaffles using butter after they are cooked and sprinkle with topping.

8 Cheese Chaffles

(Ready in about 8 minutes | Serving 2 | Difficulty: Easy)

Per serving: Kcal 208, Fat: 16g, Net Carbs: 4g, Protein: 11g

Ingredients

- 1 Egg
- 1/2 oz of Cream cheese
- 1/2 cup shredded Mozzarella cheese
- 2 1/2 tbsp of Besti Erythritol
- 2 tbsp of pumpkin puree
- 1/2 tbsp of Pumpkin pie spice
- 3 tsp of Coconut Flour

Instructions

Preheat waffle iron for around 5 minutes. Microwave cream cheese for around 30 seconds. Add the rest of the ingredients except the toppings. Pour mixture that covers the surface of the waffle maker. Cook for around 4 minutes. Take out and place on a plate and repeat with the rest of the batter.

9 Spicy Chaffles

(Ready in about 8 minutes | Serving 2 | Difficulty: Easy)

Per serving: Kcal 208, Fat: 16g, Net Carbs: 4g, Protein: 11g

Ingredients

- 1 Egg
- 1 oz of Cream cheese
- 1 cup shredded Cheddar cheese
- 1/2 tbsp of Jalapenos
- 2 tbsp of Bacon bits

Instructions

Preheat waffle iron for around 5 minutes. Microwave cream cheese for around 30 seconds. Add the rest of the ingredients except the toppings. Pour mixture that covers the surface of the waffle maker. Cook for around 4 minutes. Take out and place on a plate and repeat with the rest of the batter.

10 Double Chocolate Chaffles

(Ready in about 5 minutes | Serving 1 | Difficulty: Easy)

Per serving: Kcal 197, Fat: 23.3g, Net Carbs: 11.3g, Protein: 24.3g

Ingredients

- 1 egg
- 1 tbsp of granulated sweetener
- 1/2 cup grated mozzarella
- 1 tsp of vanilla
- 1 tbsp of chocolate chips
- 2 tbsp of almond meal/flour
- 1 tsp of heavy cream
- 2 tbsp unsweetened cocoa powder

Instructions

Add all the ingredients to a bowl and mix. Preheat the waffle maker. Spray with oil and pour half amount of batter into the maker. Cook for around 4 minutes. Sprinkle with toppings and enjoy.

11 Vanilla Chaffles

(Ready in about 10 minutes | Serving 1 | Difficulty: Easy)

Per serving: Kcal 184, Fat: 20.1g, Net Carbs: 5.4g, Protein: 22.2g

Ingredients

- 1/2 cup of grated mozzarella
- 1 tbsp of granulated sweetener
- 1 eggs
- 1 tsp of vanilla extract
- 1 tbsp of chocolate chips
- 2 tbsp of almond flour

Instructions

Combine all the ingredients in a bowl. Preheat the waffle maker and spray it using oil once it is hot. Pour half amount of batter in the maker and cook for around 4 minutes. Remove and do the same with the rest of the batter. Top and enjoy.

12 Lemon Curd Chaffle

(Ready in about 50 minutes | Serving 3 | Difficulty: Hard)

Per serving: Kcal 302, Fat: 24g, Net Carbs: 6g, Protein: 15g

Ingredients

- 3 eggs
- one batch of lemon curd
- 4 ounces softened cream cheese
- 1 tsp of vanilla extract
- 1 tbsp sweetener low carb
- 3/4 cup shredded mozzarella cheese
- 1 tsp of baking powder
- 3 tbsp of coconut flour
- 1/3 tsp of salt

Instructions

Prepare lemon curd according to package instructions. Heat the maker and spray oil. Mix baking powder, salt and coconut flour in a bowl. Add the rest of the ingredients to another bowl and beat using a hand blender. Mix the two bowls mixture and pour in the maker. Cook for around 5 minutes. Top using lemon curd.

13 Glazed Donut

(Ready in about 15 minutes | Serving 3 | Difficulty: Easy)

Per serving: Kcal 246, Fat: 17g, Net Carbs: 2g, Protein: 14g

Ingredients

For chaffles

- 1/2 cup shredded cheese Mozzarella
- 2 tbsp of whey protein
- 1 ounce of Cream Cheese
- 2 tbsp of Swerve confectioners
- 1/2tsp of Vanilla extract
- 1/2tsp of Baking powder
- 1 Egg

For glaze

- 1/2tsp of Vanilla extract
- 3-4 tbsp of Swerve confectioners
- 2 tbsp of whipping cream

Instructions

Preheat the waffle maker. Add cream cheese and mozzarella in a bowl and microwave for around 30 seconds. Add 2 tbsp sweetener, whey protein and baking powder and mix. Add dough to a bowl and break an egg into it and add vanilla. Stir to form a smooth mixture. Add batter to the waffle maker and cook for around 5 minutes. Beat glaze ingredients in a bowl and top chaffles with it.

14 Nut-Free Chaffles

(Ready in about 30 minutes | Serving 3 | Difficulty: Easy)

Per serving: Kcal 195, Fat: 15.1g, Net Carbs: 31.5g, Protein: 8.5g

Ingredients

Batter

- 1/2 cup shredded cheese mozzarella
- 1/4 tsp of vanilla extract
- 2 tbsp of SunButter
- 2 tbsp of fruit sweetener
- 1 egg
- 2 tsp of cinnamon
- 1 tbsp of coconut flour
- ⅛ tsp of baking powder

Frosting

- 1 tbsp of cream cheese
- 1/4 cup of fruit sweetener
- 3/4 tbsp of butter, melted
- 1 tbsp of coconut milk unsweetened
- 1/4 tsp of vanilla extract

Coating

- 1 tsp of fruit sweetener
- 1 tsp of cinnamon

Instructions

Preheat the waffle iron. Mix batter ingredients in a bowl and place aside. Mix frosting ingredients except for coconut milk in a bowl and whisk until smooth. Add coconut milk and mix again. Place aside. Coat iron with cooking spray and add batter. Cook for around 4 minutes. Sprinkle with sweetener and cinnamon.

15 Chicken Chaffle

(Ready in about 19 minutes | Serving 2 | Difficulty: Easy)

Per serving: Kcal 675, Fat: 52g, Net Carbs: 8g, Protein: 44g

Ingredients

- 1/4 cup of almond flour
- 1/4 cup crumbled feta cheese
- 2 eggs
- 1 tsp of baking powder
- 1/2 cup shredded chicken
- 1/4 cup of Hot Sauce
- 1/4 cup shredded mozzarella cheese
- 3/4 cup shredded cheddar cheese
- 1/4 cup diced celery

Instructions

Mix almond flour and baking powder in a bowl. Preheat iron and spray using cooking spray. Beat eggs in a bowl and add hot sauce. Combine thoroughly and pour flour mixture. Combine and add grated cheeses. Fold in chicken. Pour in the maker and cook for around 4 minutes. Top with celery and feta.

16 Chaffle Sandwich

(Ready in about 13 minutes | Serving 1 | Difficulty: Easy)

Per serving: Kcal 238, Fat: 18g, Net Carbs: 2g, Protein: 17g

Ingredients

For chaffles

- 1/2 cup shredded Cheddar cheese
- 1 egg

For sandwich

- 1 tbsp of mayonnaise
- 2 slices of tomato
- 2 strips of bacon
- 3 pieces of lettuce

Instructions

Preheat the maker and mix cheese and egg in a bowl. Pour batter into the maker and cook for around 4 minutes. Do it in 2 batches. Cook bacon in pan paced on the moderate flame until it gets crispy. Drain using paper towels and form a sandwich using tomato, mayonnaise and lettuce.

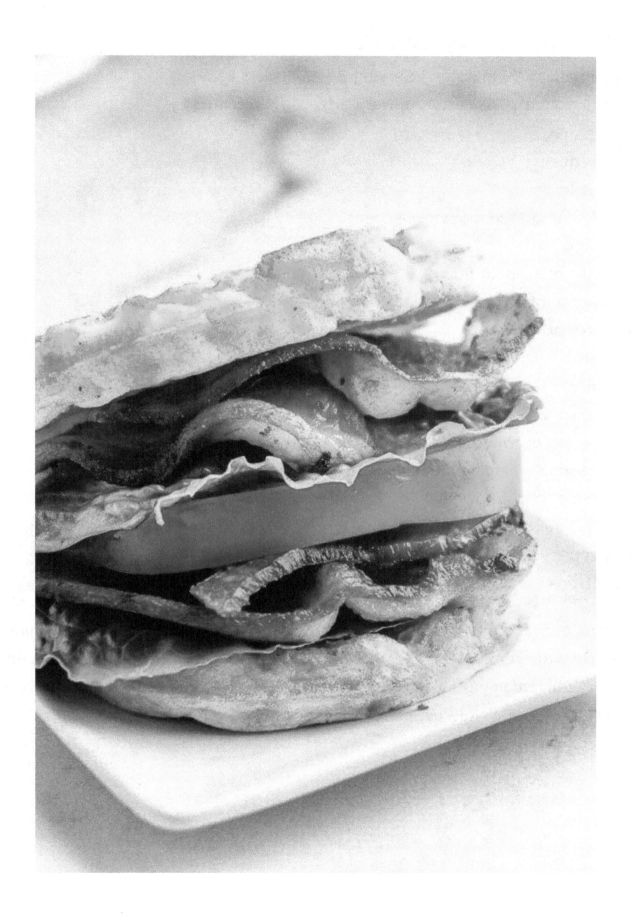

17 Sausage Gravy Chaffle

(Ready in about 15 minutes | Serving 2 | Difficulty: Easy)

Per serving: Kcal 212, Fat: 17g, Net Carbs: 3g, Protein: 11g

Ingredients

For Chaffle

- 1/2 cup grated mozzarella cheese
- 1 egg
- 1 tsp of coconut flour
- 1/4 tsp of baking powder
- 1 tsp of water
- Salt

For Gravy

- 3 tbsp of chicken broth
- 1/4 cup browned breakfast sausage
- 2 tbsp of whipping cream
- dash of garlic powder
- 2 tsp softened cream cheese
- pepper

Instructions

Preheat the maker and coat using cooking spray. Add all ingredients to a bowl and mix. Pour half amount to mixture into the maker and cook for around 4 minutes. Repeat with the remaining batter and enjoy. Prepare breakfast sausage and add in the pan with remaining ingredients and boil. Reduce flame and cook for around 7 minutes to thicken it. Add pepper and salt and spoon gravy on top of chaffles.

18 Eggs Benedict

(Ready in about 30 minutes | Serving 2 | Difficulty: Easy)

Per serving: Kcal 844, Fat: 78g, Net Carbs: 5g, Protein: 32g

Ingredients

For Chaffles

- 1/2 cup of mozzarella cheese
- 2 tbsp of almond flour
- 2 whites of eggs
- 1 tbsp of sour cream

For Hollandaise

- 2 tbsp of lemon juice
- 4 yolks of eggs
- 1/2 cup of salted butter

For Eggs

- 1 tbsp of white vinegar
- 3 ounces of deli ham
- 2 eggs

Instructions

Whisk eggs in a bowl and with the rest of the ingredients and blend. Preheat the waffle maker. Spray using cooking spray and add half the mixture. Cook for around 7 minutes. Make hollandaise sauce by forming a double broiler. Boil water and warm butter in the microwave. Add egg to bowl of the boiler. Boil and add hot butter while the pot is carried to a boil. Cook until egg thickens and take out of the bowl. Drizzle lemon juice and place aside. Warm chaffle using toaster and top with ham slices, 2 tbsp hollandaise sauce and one egg.

19 Garlic Chaffle

(Ready in about 10 minutes | Serving 8 | Difficulty: Easy)

Per serving: Kcal 74, Fat: 6.5g, Net Carbs: 0.9g, Protein: 3.4g

Ingredients

- 1 egg
- 2 tbsp of almond flour
- 1/2 cup grated mozzarella cheese
- 1/2tsp of garlic powder
- 1/2tsp of salt
- 1/2tsp of oregano

Topping

- 1/2tsp of garlic powder
- 2 tbsp softened butter
- 1/4 cup grated mozzarella cheese

Instructions

Preheat the maker and oil it. Mix ingredients except topping ingredients. Pour into the maker and cook for around 5 minutes. Mix garlic powder and butter and pour over waffle. Sprinkle with mozzarella and cook for around 3 minutes.

20 Taco Chaffle

(Ready in about 13 minutes | Serving 1 | Difficulty: Easy)

Per serving: Kcal 258, Fat: 19g, Net Carbs: 4g, Protein: 18g

Ingredients

- 1/4 cup shredded jack cheese
- 1 white of egg
- 1/4 cup shredded cheddar cheese
- 1 tsp of coconut flour
- 3/4 tsp of water
- 1/4 tsp of baking powder
- pinch of salt
- 1/8 tsp of chili powder

Instructions

Preheat the maker and oil it. Combine everything in a bowl and spoon half amount of mixture in the maker. Cook for around 4 minutes. Remove the chaffle shell and place it aside. Repeat with the remaining batter. Turn the pan and position shells of the chaffle among cups to make a shell of taco.

21 Pizza Chaffle

(Ready in about 8 minutes | Serving 2 | Difficulty: Easy)

Per serving: Kcal 76, Fat: 4.3g, Net Carbs: 4.1g, Protein: 5.5g

Ingredients

- 1 egg
- Pinch of Italian seasoning
- 1/2 cup shredded mozzarella cheese
- 1 tbsp of pizza sauce

Instructions

Preheat the maker. Whisk eggs in a bowl and add seasonings. Mix shredded cheese in a bowl. Add half amount of mixture to the maker and cook for around 4 minutes. Repeat with the rest of the batter and with 1 tbsp pizza sauce and pepperoni.

22 Parmesan Chaffles

(Ready in about 6 minutes | Serving 1 | Difficulty: Easy)

Per serving: Kcal 352, Fat: 24g, Net Carbs: 2g, Protein: 14g

Ingredients

- 1 beaten egg
- 1/2 cup of mozzarella cheese shredded
- 1/4 cup of Parmesan cheese grated
- 1/4tsp of garlic powder
- 1 tsp of Italian seasoning

Instructions

Preheat the waffle maker. Add all the ingredients except mozzarella and parmesan cheese in a bowl and mix. Mix the cheese in a bowl and spray waffle sung cooking spray. Pour half amount of mixture in the maker and cook for around 5 minutes. Top using parmesan and enjoy.

23 Italian Chaffle

(Ready in about 6 minutes | Serving 1 | Difficulty: Easy)

Per serving: Kcal 352, Fat: 24g, Net Carbs: 2g, Protein: 14g

Ingredients

- 1 beaten egg
- 1/2 cup of mozzarella cheese shredded
- 1/4 cup of Parmesan cheese grated
- 1/4tsp of garlic powder
- 1 tsp of Italian seasoning

Instructions

Preheat the waffle maker. Add all the ingredients except mozzarella and parmesan cheese in a bowl and mix. Mix the cheese in a bowl and spray waffle sung cooking spray. Pour half amount of mixture in the maker and cook for around 5 minutes. Top using parmesan and add lettuce, cold cuts, tomato.

24 Chaffle Breadsticks

(Ready in about 6 minutes | Serving 1 | Difficulty: Easy)

Per serving: Kcal 352, Fat: 24g, Net Carbs: 2g, Protein: 14g

Ingredients

- 1 beaten egg
- 1/2 cup of mozzarella cheese shredded
- Marinara sauce
- 1/4 cup of Parmesan cheese grated
- 1/4tsp of garlic powder
- 1 tsp of Italian seasoning

Instructions

Preheat the waffle maker. Add all the ingredients except mozzarella and parmesan cheese in a bowl and mix. Mix the cheese in a bowl and spray waffle sung cooking spray. Pour half amount of mixture in the maker and cook for around 5 minutes. Top using parmesan and dice into 4 sticks and enjoy with Marinara Sauce.

25 Chaffle Bruschetta

(Ready in about 6 minutes | Serving 1 | Difficulty: Easy)

Per serving: Kcal 352, Fat: 24g, Net Carbs: 2g, Protein: 14g

Ingredients

- 1 beaten egg
- 1/2 cup of mozzarella cheese shredded
- 1/4 cup of Parmesan cheese grated
- Basil
- Olive oil
- 1/4tsp of garlic powder
- 1 tsp of Italian seasoning

Instructions

Preheat the waffle maker. Add all the ingredients except mozzarella and parmesan cheese in a bowl and mix. Mix the cheese in a bowl and spray waffle sung cooking spray. Pour half amount of mixture in the maker and cook for around 5 minutes. Top using parmesan and mix 4 chopped cherry tomatoes, ½ tsp chopped fresh basil, drop of olive oil and salt. Add on chaffle.

26 Cauliflower Chaffles

(Ready in about 9 minutes | Serving 2 | Difficulty: Easy)

Per serving: Kcal 246, Fat: 16g, Net Carbs: 7g, Protein: 20g

Ingredients

- 1/4 tsp of Garlic Powder
- 1 cup of riced cauliflower
- 1/4 tsp of Ground Black Pepper
- 1/4 tsp of Kosher Salt
- 1/2 tsp of Italian seasoning
- 1 Eggs
- 1/2 cup of mozzarella cheese shredded
- 1/2 cup of parmesan cheese shredded

Instructions

Blend all ingredients except the cauliflower mixture and parmesan cheese in a blender and sprinkle half parmesan in the maker. Pour mixture in maker and top with cauliflower mixture and rest of parmesan. Cook for around 5 minutes.

27 Zucchini Chaffles

(Ready in about 15 minutes | Serving 2 | Difficulty: Easy)

Per serving: Kcal 194, Fat: 13g, Net Carbs: 4g, Protein: 16g

Ingredients

- 1 beaten Egg
- 1/2 tsp Black Pepper Ground
- 1 cup grated Zucchini
- 1/2 cup of parmesan cheese shredded
- 1 tsp chopped Dried Basil
- 1/4 cup of mozzarella cheese shredded
- 3/4 tsp divided Kosher Salt

Instructions

Sprinkle 1/4 tsp salt on zucchini. Beat egg in a bowl and add mozzarella, zucchini, 1/2 tsp salt, basil and pepper. Sprinkle 2 tbsp parmesan on iron and spread a quarter of zucchini mixture on the maker. Top using 2 tbsp parmesan and cook for around 8 minutes. Repeat with the rest of the mixture.

28 Peanut Chaffles

(Ready in about 6 minutes | Serving 2 | Difficulty: Easy)

Per serving: Kcal 264, Fat: 21.6g, Net Carbs: 7.25g, Protein: 9.45g

Ingredients

Chaffle

- 1 Egg
- 1/4 tsp of Baking Powder
- 1 tbsp of Unsweetened Cocoa
- 1 tbsp of Heavy Cream
- 1 tbsp of Powdered Sweetener
- 1/2 tsp of Vanilla Extract
- 1 tsp of Coconut Flour
- 1/2 tsp of Batter Flavor

Butter Filling

- 2 tsp of Powdered Sweetener
- 3 tbsp of Peanut Butter
- 2 tbsp of Heavy Cream

InstructionsPreheat the maker. Combine ingredients of chaffle in a bowl and pour half amount of mixture in maker. Cook for around 5 minutes. Repeat with the rest of the mixture. Blend butter ingredients and spread over chaffles.

29 Easy Chaffle Recipe

(Ready in about 10 minutes | Serving 2| Difficulty: Easy)

Ingredients
Simple Chaffles

Per serving: Kcal 152, Fat: 8g, Net Carbs: 1g, Protein: 9g

- 1 Egg
- 1/2 Cup of Shredded Cheese Mozarella

Instructions

Add all ingredients to a bowl and whisk to combine. Coat waffle maker using cooking spray and pour half amount of batter into the maker. Cook for around 5 minutes and repeat with the rest of the batter.

30 Savory Chaffles

Per serving: Kcal 215, Fat: 16.5g, Net Carbs: 2g, Protein: 12g

- 1 Egg
- 1/2 Cup Shredded Cheese Mozarella
- 1/16 Tsp of Xanthan Gum
- 1/4 Cup of Almond Flour

Instructions

Add all ingredients to a bowl and whisk to combine. Coat waffle maker using cooking spray and pour half amount of batter into the maker. Cook for around 5 minutes and repeat with the rest of the batter.

31 Sweet Chaffles

Per serving: Kcal 192, Fat: 15gg, Net Carbs: 1.55g, Protein: 15g

- 1 Egg
- 1/2 Cup of Shredded Cheese Mozzarella
- 1/4 Cup of Almond Flour
- 1/16 Tsp of Xanthan Gum
- 2 Tbsp of Confectioners Swerve

Instructions

Add all ingredients to a bowl and whisk to combine. Coat waffle maker using cooking spray and pour half amount of batter into the maker. Cook for around 5 minutes and repeat with the rest of the batter.

32 Tasty Chaffles

(Ready in about 13 minutes | Serving 2 | Difficulty: Easy)

Per serving: Kcal 116, Fat: 9.5gg, Net Carbs: 2.6g, Protein: 4.5g

Ingredients

- 1 oz softened cream cheese
- 1 tbsp of almond flour
- 1 tbsp of pumpkin puree
- 1 egg
- 1/2 tsp of pumpkin spice

Instructions

Whisk the cream cheese in a bowl. Whisk pumpkin puree and egg in a bowl. Add almond flour and pumpkin spice and mix. Preheat the iron and spray using oil. Pour half amount of mixture in the maker and cook for around 5 minutes. Repeat with the rest of the batter.

33 Bread Sticks Chaffle

(Ready in about 12 minutes | Serving 7 | Difficulty: Easy)

Per serving: Kcal 80, Fat: 7g, Net Carbs: 1g, Protein: 5g

Ingredients

- 1 egg
- 2 tbsp of almond flour
- 1/2 cup grated mozzarella cheese
- 1/2tsp of garlic powder
- 1/2tsp of salt
- 1/2tsp of oregano

Topping

- 1/2tsp of garlic powder
- 2 tbsp softened butter
- 1/4 cup grated mozzarella cheese

Instructions

Preheat the maker and oil it. Mix all ingredients except topping ingredients. Pour in the maker and cook for around 5 minutes. Make four strips of waffle. Mix butter and garlic powder and coat strips with it. Sprinkle with mozzarella and cook for around 3 minutes.

34 Original Chaffle

(Ready in about 5 minutes | Serving 1 | Difficulty: Easy)

Per serving: Kcal 246, Fat: 18g, Net Carbs: 2g, Protein: 17g

Ingredients

- 2 eggs
- 1/4 cup of almond flour
- 1/2 cup of mozzarella
- 1/2 tsp of baking powder

Instructions

Preheat iron and spray with cooking spray. Mix all the ingredients in a bowl and pour half amount of the mixture into the maker. Cook for around 5 minutes and repeat with the rest of the mixture.

35 Mini Chaffles

(Ready in about 11 minutes | Serving 2 | Difficulty: Easy)

Per serving: Kcal 73, Fat: 6g, Net Carbs: 4g, Protein: 2g

Ingredients

- 2 tsp of Coconut Flour
- 1/4 tsp of Baking Powder
- 4 tsp of Swerve
- 1 Egg
- 1/2 tsp of Vanilla Extract
- 1 oz of Cream Cheese

Instructions

Preheat the iron. Add baking powder, coconut flour and swerve in a bowl and mix. Add cream cheese, egg and vanilla extract in bowl and mix. Pour mixture in the maker and cook for around 4 minutes.

36 Grain-free chaffles

(Ready in about 20 minutes | Serving 2 | Difficulty: Easy)

Per serving: Kcal 277, Fat: 20g, Net Carbs: 4.6g, Protein: 4.8g

Ingredients

- 1 tbsp of almond flour
- 1 tsp of vanilla
- 1 egg
- 1 shake of cinnamon
- 1 cup of mozzarella cheese
- 1 tsp of baking powder
- Butter

Instructions

Mix vanilla extract and egg in a bowl. Mix almond flour, baking powder and cinnamon. Add mozzarella cheese at the end and coat with the mixture evenly. Spray waffle using oil and turn it on. Pour mixture and cook for around 5 minutes. Top with butter and enjoy.

37 Healthy Chaffles

(Ready in about 20 minutes | Serving 4 | Difficulty: Easy)

Per serving: Kcal 411, Fat: 35g, Net Carbs: 6g, Protein: 21g

Ingredients

- 1 1/2 cup of shredded cheese cheddar
- 4 oz. cream cheese
- 4 eggs
- 2 tsp of baking powder
- 1/2 cup of almond flour
- Syrup

Instructions

Oil the waffle maker and mix all ingredients in a bowl. Pour batter into the maker and cook for around 5 minutes. Top with syrup(sugar-free) and enjoy.

38 Sunny Chaffle

(Ready in about 10 minutes | Serving 1 | Difficulty: Easy)

Per serving: Kcal 320, Fat: 24.3g, Net Carbs: 3.1g, Protein: 21.7g

Ingredients

- 1 egg
- Strawberries
- 2 tbsp of almond flour
- 1/2 cup of mozzarella cheese
- 1/2tsp of baking powder

Instructions

Preheat the maker and mix all the ingredients in a bowl. Pour into the center of the maker and cook for around 5 minutes. Top with strawberries and enjoy.

39 Traditional Chaffles

(Ready in about 13 minutes | Serving 1 | Difficulty: Easy)

Per serving: Kcal 291, Fat: 23g, Net Carbs: 1g, Protein: 20g

Ingredients

- 1/2 cup of shredded cheese cheddar
- 1 egg

Instructions

Preheat the maker and oil it gently. Break the egg in a bowl and add the half cup of cheddar cheese. Mix and pour half amount of mixture in maker. Cook for around 4 minutes. Repeat with the rest of the mixture.

40 Best Pizza Chaffle

(Ready in about 20 minutes | Serving 2 | Difficulty: Easy)

Per serving: Kcal 241, Fat: 18g, Net Carbs: 4g, Protein: 17g

Ingredients

- 1 tsp of coconut flour
- 1/2 cup of shredded cheese mozzarella
- 1 white of egg
- `1 tsp softened cream cheese
- 1/8 tsp of Italian seasoning
- 1/4 tsp of baking powder
- 1/8 tsp of garlic powder
- 3 tsp of marinara sauce
- Salt
- 1/2 cup of mozzarella cheese
- 1 tbsp shredded cheese parmesan
- 6 pepperonis diced in half
- 1/4 tsp of basil seasoning

Instructions

Preheat the oven to 400 degrees F. Preheat the maker as well. Add all the ingredients except pepperoni and parmesan cheese in a bowl and mix. Pour half amount of mixture in the maker and cook for around 4 minutes. Repeat with the rest of the mixture. Top with pepperoni, tomato sauce and parmesan cheese. Bake in the oven by placing on the top shelf for around 6 minutes. Turn broil setting and cook for around 2 minutes. Sprinkle with basil.

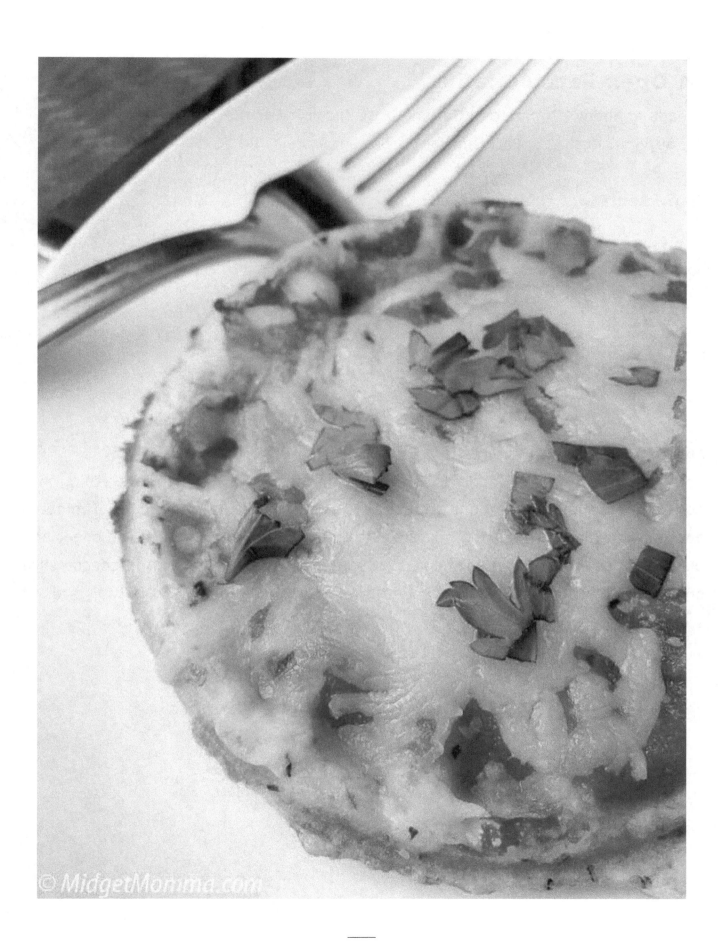

41 Open-Faced Chaffle

(Ready in about 17 minutes | Serving 2 | Difficulty: Easy)

Per serving: Kcal 118, Fat: 8g, Net Carbs: 2g, Protein: 9g

Ingredients

- 1 egg only white
- 1/4 cup shredded cheddar cheese
- 1/4 cup shredded cheese mozzarella
- 3/4 tsp of water
- 1/4 tsp of baking powder
- 1 tsp of coconut flour
- Salt

Instructions

Preheat the oven to 425 degrees F. Preheat the maker as well. Mix everything in a bowl and pour half the amount of mixture into a maker. Cook for around 4 minutes and repeat with the remaining mixture. Line parchment paper on a cookie sheet and place chaffles on it. Add a quarter cup of roasted keto beef gravy. Add cheese slice on top and bake in the oven for around 5 minutes in the top rack. Broil for around 1 minute.

42 Cream Chaffles

(Ready in about 15 minutes | Serving 2 | Difficulty: Easy)

Per serving: Kcal 293, Fat: 27g, Net Carbs: 5g, Protein: 10g

Ingredients

- 4 eggs
- 1 tsp of vanilla extract
- 2 tbsp of melted butter
- 4 oz of cream cheese
- 1 tsp of baking powder

Instructions

Blend all ingredients in a blender for around 1 minute. Spray the waffle maker using cooking spray and pour the mixture into the maker. Cook until it turns crispy and golden.

43 Fluffy Chaffles

(Ready in about 45 minutes | Serving 8 | Difficulty: Moderate)

Per serving: Kcal 140, Fat: 11g, Net Carbs: 4g, Protein: 4g

Ingredients

- 64 g of almond flour
- 1 1/2 tsp of baking powder
- 1 tbsp of ground psyllium husk
- 28 g of coconut flour
- 1 tsp of xanthan gum
- 57 g of butter
- 240 ml of water
- 3 tbsp of erythritol
- 3 eggs beaten
- 1/4 tsp of kosher salt
- 1 tsp of vanilla extract

Instructions

Mix flours, xantham gum and husk in a bowl. Warm water, sweetener, salt and butter in a pot and once it starts simmering, add flours and incorporate. Cook for around 3 minutes. Transfer dough to bowl and add egg one by one, mixing using an electric mixer. Add baking powder and vanilla extract and mix. Heat the maker and oil it. Pour batter and cook for around 12 minutes.

44 Almond Flour Chaffles

(Ready in about 20 minutes | Serving 2 | Difficulty: Easy)

Per serving: Kcal 70, Fat: 3.8g, Net Carbs: 4.9g, Protein: 4g

Ingredients

- 4 separated eggs
- 1/4 cup of granulated Swerve
- 2 cup of almond flour
- 2 tsp of baking powder
- 1/2 cup of butter
- 1 tsp of kosher salt
- 1/2 cup of almond butter
- Cooking spray
- 2 tsp. of vanilla extract
- Maple syrup

Instructions

Preheat waffle maker to high. Mix stevia, almond flour, salt and baking powder in a bowl. Melt almond butter and butter in the microwave for around 15 seconds. Stir dry ingredients with butter mixture and then add vanilla and yolks. Beat whites in a separate bowl and fold in batter. Spray maker using cooking spray and pour the batter. Cook for around 5 minutes. Top with maple syrup and butter.

45 Butter Chaffles

(Ready in about 30 minutes | Serving 5 | Difficulty: Easy)

Per serving: Kcal 216, Fat: 19.9g, Net Carbs: 5.5g, Protein: 6.4g

Ingredients

- 5 eggs
- 4 tbsp of granulated sweetener
- 4 tbsp of coconut flour
- 1 tsp of baking powder
- 3 tbsp of milk full fat
- 2 tsp of vanilla
- 125 g of butter melted

Instructions

Beat egg whites in a bowl. Mix yolks with sweetener, baking powder and coconut flour in a separate bowl. Add butter and mix. Add vanilla and milk and mix. Fold whites in yolk mixture and pour in maker. Cook for around 5 minutes.

46 Paleo Chaffles

(Ready in about 10minutes | Serving 2 | Difficulty: Easy)

Per serving: Kcal 401, Fat: 37, Net Carbs: 9g, Protein: 13g

Ingredients

- 1 egg
- 2 tbsp of sweetener
- 1/2 cup of Almond Flour
- 1/2 tsp of baking powder Gluten-free
- 2 tbsp of Almond butter
- 1/4 tsp of Sea salt
- 2 tbsp of Butter
- 1/2 tsp of Vanilla extract
- 1/4 cup of almond milk Unsweetened

Instructions

Preheat waffle maker to high temperature. Oil it gently and beat whites in a bowl. Combine baking powder, erythritol, salt and almond flour in another bowl. Melt almond butter and butter in the microwave and add to the flour mixture. Add yolk, vanilla and almond milk and stir. Fold whites in batter and mix. Pour in the maker and cook for around 5 minutes.

47 Crispy Chaffles

(Ready in about 10 minutes | Serving 4 | Difficulty: Easy)

Per serving: Kcal 64, Fat: 2g, Net Carbs: 4g, Protein: 5g

Ingredients

- 4 tbsp sifted coconut flour
- 1/4 tsp of baking powder
- 1 tsp of coconut oil
- 1 tbsp sweetener granulated
- 2/3 cup of egg whites
- 1/2 tsp of vanilla extract
- 1/4 cup of milk
- 1 tbsp of unsweetened apple sauce

Instructions

Mix sweetener, baking powder and coconut flour in a bowl. Add whites, vanilla, apple sauce and milk in a separate bowl and mix. Pour to the other bowl and form a thick batter. Add oil and spray waffle maker using cooking spray. Once the maker is hot, pour the batter and cook for around 4 minutes.

48 Salted Chaffles

(Ready in about 15 minutes | Serving 2 | Difficulty: Easy)

Per serving: Kcal 425, Fat: 36.7g, Net Carbs: 10.7g, Protein: 14.8g

Ingredients

Dry

- 3/4 cup of Almond Flour
- 1 tbsp of Coconut flour
- 2 tbsp of Erythritol
- 1 tsp of Baking Powder
- 1/8 tsp of Himalayan Salt

Wet

- 2 tbsp of Melted Butter
- 2 Eggs
- 2 tbsp of Cream Cheese at room temperature
- 1 tsp of Vanilla Extract

Instructions

Preheat waffle maker to high. Mix wet ingredients in a bowl. Mix dry ingredients in a separate bowl. Mix both bowls and pour in the maker. Cook for around 4 minutes.

49 Low Carb Chaffles

(Ready in about 8 minutes | Serving 1 | Difficulty: Easy)

Per serving: Kcal 522, Fat: 48g, Net Carbs: 7g, Protein: 19g

Ingredients

- 2 eggs
- 1/2 tsp of baking powder
- 4 tbsp of almond flour
- 2 oz of cream cheese
- 1 tbsp of coconut oil

Instructions

Blend everything in the blender and pour in the maker, which is oiled. Cook for around 3 minutes.

50 Sweet Chaffles

(Ready in about 9 minutes | Serving 2 | Difficulty: Easy)

Per serving: Kcal 331, Fat: 29g, Net Carbs: 7g, Protein: 11g

Ingredients

Dry

- 1/2 cup of almond flour
- 1/2 tsp of sweetener
- 1/4tsp of baking soda
- 1/4tsp of salt
- 1/4 tsp of baking powder
- 1/8 tsp of nutmeg
- 1/4tsp of ground cinnamon
- 1/8 tsp of cloves

Wet

- 2 eggs
- 2 tbsp of melted butter
- 1 tsp of vanilla extract

Instructions

Add dry ingredients to a bowl and mix. Separate yolks and whites in two bowls and mix butter and vanilla in yolks. Beat whites and add yolks to dry ingredients. Then add whites while mixing gently. Preheat maker to high temperature and pour the mixture. Cook for around 5 minutes.

©MidgetMomma.com

51 Churro Chaffle

(Ready in about 15 minutes | Serving 1 | Difficulty: Easy)

Per serving: Kcal 193, Fat: 14g, Net Carbs: 2g, Protein: 8g

Ingredients

- 1 egg
- 1/4 cup of almond flour
- 1 tsp of cinnamon
- 1/2 cup of shredded cheese mozzarella
- 2 tbsp of Swerve granular
- 2 tbsp of melted butter
- ⅛ tsp of baking powder
- 3 tbsp of Swerve granular

Instructions

Combine everything in a bowl and pour the mixture into the maker by dividing it into three parts. Melt butter in the meantime in a pan over moderate flame. Add churro toppings and enjoy.

52 Avocado Egg Bake

(Ready in about 20 minutes | Serving 1 | Difficulty: Easy)

Per serving: Kcal 605, Fat: 50.9g, Net Carbs: 18.6g, Protein: 25.3g

Ingredients

- 2 eggs
- 1 avocado, pitted and halved
- ¼ cup of shredded Cheddar cheese
- 1 tbsp. chopped fresh parsley, or according to taste
- Freshly ground black pepper and salt according to taste

Instructions

- Preheat oven to 425 degrees Fahrenheit.
- To make way for one egg, scoop out some of the avocados from where the pit. Put each avocado half on the baking sheet, then crack one egg on top.
- Cook for fifteen to twenty minutes in a preheated oven before the egg is ready. Season with pepper and salt and finish with Cheddar cheese. Serve with new parsley as a garnish.

53 Oven-Baked Bacon

(Ready in about 35 minutes | Serving 6 | Difficulty: Easy)

Per serving: Kcal 134, Fat: 10.4g, Net Carbs: 0.4g, Protein: 9.2g

Ingredients

1 (16 oz.) package bacon

Instructions

- Preheat oven to 350°F. Using parchment paper, line a baking dish.
- Put the bacon slices on a prepared baking sheet, one on top of the other.
- Bake for fifteen to twenty minutes in a preheated oven. Take off the dish from the oven. Return the bacon slices to the oven after tossing them with kitchen tongs. Bake for another fifteen to twenty minutes, or till crispy. Thinner slices may require less time to cook, about twenty minutes overall. Drain on a paper towel-lined pan.

54 Roasted Leeks With Eggs

(Ready in about 40 minutes | Serving 2 | Difficulty: Easy)

Per serving: Kcal 1219, Fat: 124.6g, Net Carbs: 27.8g, Protein: 11.8g

Ingredients

- 3 green onions
- 2 leeks
- 2 tbsp. melted ghee (clarified butter)
- ¼ tsp. ground black pepper
- ½ tsp. sea salt

Avocado Vinaigrette:

- ¾ cup of light olive oil
- ⅛ tsp. red pepper flakes
- 1 ripe avocado, flesh scooped from the skin, pitted
- 1 lemon, juiced
- Ground black pepper and salt according to taste
- ¼ cup of red wine vinegar
- 1 tsp. olive oil
- ¼ cup of sliced, toasted almonds
- 2 eggs

Instructions

- Preheat oven to 400 degrees Fahrenheit.
- Green tops and bottom half-inch of the leeks should be discarded. Leeks can be sliced in half lengthwise.
- On a sheet tray, arrange the green onions and leeks. Drizzle ghee on top. Season with salt and pepper.
- For fifteen to twenty minutes in a preheated oven, roast till brown.
- In a food processor, thoroughly 3/4 cup olive oil, mix avocado, vinegar, lemon juice, pepper, and salt to make the vinaigrette

- In a skillet on medium-low flame, heat 1 tsp. oil for two to three minutes, or before whites are just set and the yolks are already runny, break eggs onto the opposite sides of the skillet.
- Remove the leeks and onions from the oven and put them on top with the sunny-side-up eggs. On top, sprinkle red pepper flakes and almonds. Finish with an avocado vinaigrette drizzle.

55 Gluten-Free Bagels

(Ready in about 30 minutes | Serving 6 | Difficulty: Easy)

Per serving: Kcal 364, Fat: 27.9g, Net Carbs: 9.7g, Protein: 20.9g

Ingredients

- 1 tbsp. baking powder, gluten-free
- 1 ½ cups of almond flour
- 2 eggs
- 1 tsp. garlic salt
- 2 oz. cream cheese, cubed
- 2 ½ cups of shredded mozzarella cheese

Instructions

- Preheat oven to 400 degrees Fahrenheit. Using parchment paper, line the baking sheet.
- In a mixing bowl, add the baking powder, garlic salt, and almond flour.
- In the microwave-safe bowl, mix mozzarella and cream cheese. Microwave for one minute, then remove and mix. Microwave for another minute, then take it off and stir until all is well combined. Working fast, stir the eggs and flour mixture into melted cheese mixture. Knead the dough by hand until it becomes a sticky dough. Continue kneading and pressing the dough for approximately two minutes or until it is fully uniform.
- The dough can be divided into six equal bits. Roll each one into the long log, then push the ends together to form a bagel shape and put it on the baking sheet that has been prepared.
- For ten to fourteen minutes in the preheated oven, bake till the bagels are golden.

55 Keto Zucchini Hash

(Ready in about 30 minutes | Serving 4 | Difficulty: Easy)

Per serving: Kcal 200, Fat: 17.9g, Net Carbs: 5g, Protein: g

Ingredients

- 3 tbsp. coconut oil
- 4 small zucchini, squeezed dry and grated
- 1 tbsp. butter
- 1 tsp. chili powder, or according to taste
- ⅓ cup of grated Parmesan cheese
- 1 tsp. sea salt
- 2 eggs, beaten
- 1 tsp. cayenne pepper (Optional)

Directions

- In a small skillet over medium flame, combine the coconut oil, butter, and zucchini. Add the chili powder, Parmesan cheese, cayenne pepper, and salt to a mixing bowl. Stir until the cheese has melted.
- Reduce the heat to a minimum and whisk in the eggs before thoroughly combined. Adjust to medium heat and fry, stirring and tossing sometimes, for almost fifteen minutes, or till the edges of hash are lightly browned.

Keto Smoothies And Shakes

1 Triple berry smoothie

(Ready in about 2 minutes | Serving 1 | Difficulty: Easy)

Per serving: Kcal 330, Fat: 26g, Net Carbs: 21g, Protein: 12g

Ingredients

- 2 tbsp of hemp seeds
- 1 cup of water
- Half avocado
- 1/2 cup of frozen berries (raspberries, blueberries, and strawberries)
- 2 cups of spinach

Instructions

Add everything to a blender and turn it on. Blend until smooth and enjoy.

2 Chocolate smoothie

(Ready in about 2 minutes | Serving 1 | Difficulty: Easy)

Per serving: Kcal 345, Fat: 31g, Net Carbs: 13g, Protein: 11

ingredients

- 1 cup of almond milk unsweetened
- 2 tbsp of peanut butter
- 1/4 cup of heavy cream
- 1 tbsp of cocoa powder unsweetened
- 1 cup of ice

Instructions

Add everything to a blender and turn it on. Blend until smooth and enjoy.

3 Zucchini smoothie

(Ready in about 2 minutes | Serving 1 | Difficulty: Easy)

Per serving: Kcal 219, Fat: 12g, Net Carbs: 24g, Protein: 7g

Ingredients

- 1 cup of zucchini chopped
- 1 cup of water
- 3 tbsp of chia seeds
- 1/2 cup of frozen strawberries

Instructions

Add everything to a blender and turn it on. Blend until smooth and enjoy.

4 Coconut smoothie

(Ready in about 2 minutes | Serving 1 | Difficulty: Easy)

Per serving: Kcal 321, Fat: 29g, Net Carbs: 17g, Protein: 4g

Ingredients

- 1/2 cup of full-fat unsweetened coconut milk
- 1/2 cup of blackberries frozen
- 10 mint leaves
- 2 tbsp of coconut shredded

Instructions

Add everything to a blender and turn it on. Blend until smooth and enjoy.

5 Lemon smoothie

(Ready in about 2 minutes | Serving 1 | Difficulty: Easy)

Per serving: Kcal 100, Fat: 6g, Net Carbs: 10g, Protein: 4g

Ingredients

- 1/2 cup of water
- 1 cup sliced cucumber
- 1/2 cup of ice
- 1 cup of spinach or kale
- 2 tbsp of flax seeds
- 1 tbsp of lemon juice

Instructions

Add everything to a blender and turn it on. Blend until smooth and enjoy.

6 Cinnamon smoothie

(Ready in about 2 minutes | Serving 1 | Difficulty: Easy)

Per serving: Kcal 286, Fat: 21g, Net Carbs: 19g, Protein: 10g

Ingredients

- 1 cup of almond milk unsweetened
- 1/8 tsp of cinnamon
- 1 cup of spinach
- 1/2 cup of raspberries frozen
- 2 tbsp of almond butter

Instructions

Add everything to a blender and turn it on. Blend until smooth and enjoy.

© www.whatscookingwithruthie.com

7 Strawberry smoothie

(Ready in about 2 minutes | Serving 1 | Difficulty: Easy)

Per serving: Kcal 431, Fat: 43g, Net Carbs: 10g, Protein: 4g

Ingredients

- 1/2 cup of water
- 1/2 cup of strawberries frozen
- 1/2 cup of heavy cream

Instructions

Add everything to a blender and turn it on. Blend until smooth and enjoy.

8 Cauliflower smoothie

(Ready in about 2 minutes | Serving 1 | Difficulty: Easy)

Per serving: Kcal 308, Fat: 23g, Net Carbs: 19g, Protein: 15g

Ingredients

- 1 cup of almond unsweetened
- 1 cup of cauliflower florets frozen
- 1.5 tbsp of cocoa powder unsweetened
- 1 tbsp of cacao nibs
- 3 tbsp of hemp seeds
- Sea salt

Instructions

Add everything to a blender and turn it on. Blend until smooth and enjoy.

9 Pumpkin smoothie

(Ready in about 2 minutes | Serving 1 | Difficulty: Easy)

Per serving: Kcal 462, Fat: 42g, Net Carbs: 19g, Protein: 10g

Ingredients

- 1/2 cup of coconut milk unsweetened
- 1/2 cup of ice
- 2 tbsp of almond butter
- 1/2 cup of pumpkin purée
- 1/4 tsp of pie spice pumpkin
- Sea salt

Instructions

Add everything to a blender and turn it on. Blend until smooth and enjoy.

10 Lime pie smoothie

(Ready in about 2 minutes | Serving 1 | Difficulty: Easy)

Per serving: Kcal 281, Fat: 23g, Net Carbs: 17g, Protein: 8g

Ingredients

- 1 cup of water
- 1/4 cup of raw cashews
- 1/2 cup of almond milk unsweetened
- 1 cup of spinach
- 2 tbsp of lime juice
- 2 tbsp of coconut shredded

Instructions

Add everything to a blender and turn it on. Blend until smooth and enjoy.

11 Coconut Smoothie

(Ready in about 5 minutes | Serving 1 | Difficulty: Easy)

Per serving: Kcal 500, Fat: 38g, Net Carbs: 8g, Protein: 26g

Ingredients

- 3/4 cup canned coconut milk full-fat
- Handful of ice
- 2 tbsp cacao powder unsweetened
- 15 drops of liquid stevia coconut
- 2 scoops of collagen protein

Instructions

Add everything to the blender except collagen and turn it on. Blend until smooth and add collagen. Blend again and enjoy.

12 Cinnamon Smoothie

(Ready in about 5 minutes | Serving 1 | Difficulty: Easy)

Per serving: Kcal 300, Fat: 30g, Net Carbs: 14g, Protein: 3g

Ingredients

- 3/4 cup of coconut milk
- 2 tsp cacao powder unsweetened
- 1/2 ripe avocado
- 1 tsp of cinnamon powder
- Stevia
- 1/4 tsp of vanilla extract

Instructions

Add everything to a blender and turn it on. Blend until smooth and enjoy.

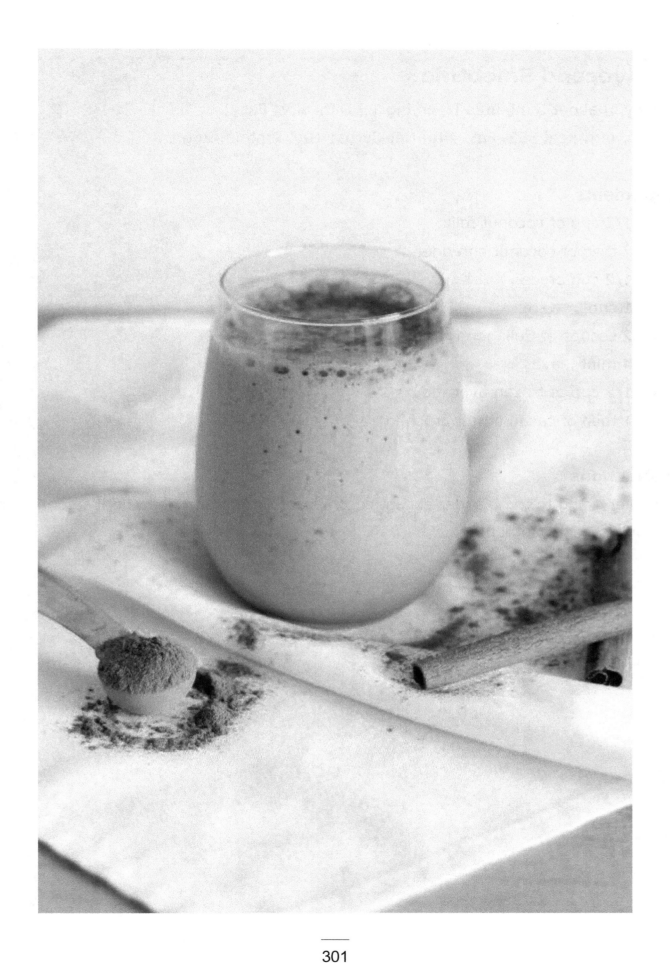

13 Avocado Smoothie

(Ready in about 5 minutes | Serving 1 | Difficulty: Easy)

Per serving: Kcal 552, Fat: 44g, Net Carbs: 10g, Protein: 26g

Ingredients

- 1/2 cup of coconut milk
- 2 tbsp of coconut shredded
- 1/2 cup of ice
- 1 cup of water
- 2 scoops of Collagen Protein Chocolate
- 4 mint leaves
- 1/2 cup of frozen avocado
- 1 tbsp of cacao butter crushed

Instructions

Add everything to the blender except coconut and turn it on. Blend until smooth and top with coconut and enjoy.

14 Keto Smoothie

(Ready in about 5 minutes | Serving 2 | Difficulty: Easy)

Per serving: Kcal 148, Fat: 11g, Net Carbs: 13g, Protein: 2g

Ingredients

- 1 cup of cold water
- 1/2 cup of cilantro
- 1 cup of baby spinach
- 1 inch peeled ginger
- 1/2-1 peeled lemon
- 3/4 English peeled cucumber
- 1 cup avocado frozen

Instructions

Add everything to a blender and turn it on. Blend until smooth and enjoy.

15 Cucumber Smoothie

(Ready in about 5 minutes | Serving 2 | Difficulty: Easy)

Per serving: Kcal 69, Fat: 4.6g, Net Carbs: 6.8g, Protein: 2g

Ingredients

- 8 ounces of water
- 1 cup cucumber sliced
- 2 tsp of Tea powder Match Green
- 2 ounces of ripe avocado
- 1/2 tsp of liquid stevia lemon
- 1 tsp of lemon juice
- 1/2 cup of ice

Instructions

Blend tea powder and water first, and then add the rest of the ingredients. Blend and enjoy.

16 Kale Shake

(Ready in about 5 minutes | Serving 1 | Difficulty: Easy)

Per serving: Kcal 141, Fat: 10.8g, Net Carbs: 8.6g, Protein: 4g

Ingredients

- 1 cup almond milk unsweetened
- 4 cups kale chopped
- 1/2 cup canned full-fat coconut milk
- 1/4 cup coconut ground
- 1/4 tsp of kosher salt
- 1 1-inch fresh ginger piece, peeled
- 1 cup of ice

Instructions

Add coconut milk first, and then almond, followed by the rest of the ingredients in a blender and turn it on. Blend until smooth and enjoy.

17 Turmeric Smoothie

(Ready in about 2 minutes | Serving 1 | Difficulty: Easy)

Per serving: Kcal 600, Fat: 56g, Net Carbs: 6g, Protein: 7g

Ingredients

- 200 ml coconut milk full fat
- 1 tbsp of Chia seeds
- 1 tsp of granulated sweetener
- 200 ml almond milk unsweetened
- 1 tbsp of ground turmeric
- 1 tsp of ground ginger
- 1 tsp of ground cinnamon
- 1 tbsp of MCT Oil

Instructions

Add everything except chia seeds to the blender and turn it on. Blend until smooth and top with seeds and enjoy.

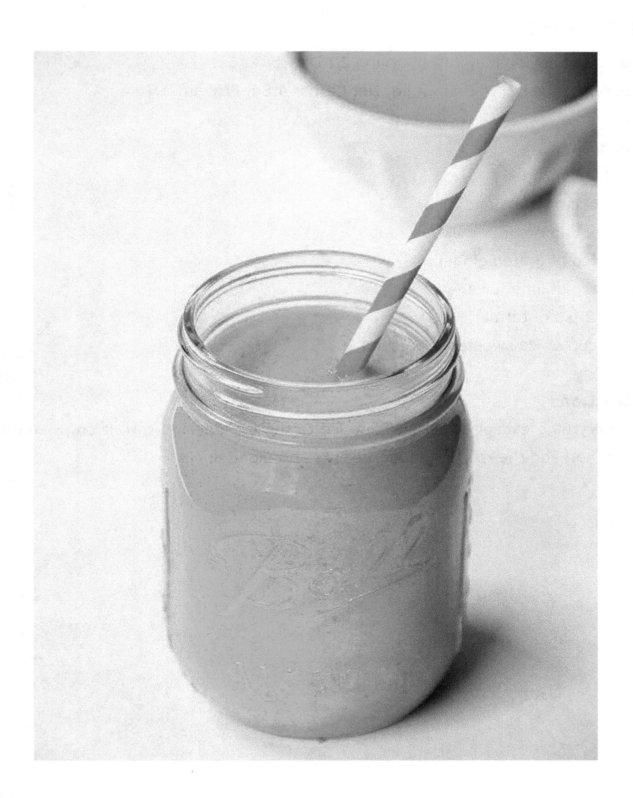

18 Ginger Smoothie

(Ready in about 10 minutes | Serving 2 | Difficulty: Easy)

Per serving: Kcal 232, Fat: 22.4g, Net Carbs: 4.8g, Protein: 1.7g

Ingredients

- 1/2 avocado
- 1/4 cup of almond milk
- 3/4 cup coconut milk full - fat
- 1 tsp of grated ginger
- 1 tsp of lime juice
- 1/2 tsp of turmeric
- 1 cup of ice sweetener crushed

Instructions

Add everything except sweetener and ice to the blender and turn it on. Blend until smooth and add the rest of the ingredients and blend again.

19 Paleo Smoothie

(Ready in about 5 minutes | Serving 2 | Difficulty: Easy)

Per serving: Kcal 387, Fat: 25g, Net Carbs: 12g, Protein: 27g

Ingredients

- 1 cup of water
- stevia
- 1/2 cup of coconut milk full-fat
- 1 scraped gluten-free vanilla bean
- 2 tbsp of collagen hydrolysate
- 3 cups of ice
- 2 tbsp of golden flax ground

Instructions

Add everything to the blender and turn it on. Blend until smooth and enjoy.

20 Post Workout Smoothie

(Ready in about 3minutes | Serving 1 | Difficulty: Easy)

Per serving: Kcal 474, Fat: 21g, Net Carbs: 54g, Protein: 27g

Ingredients

- 1 cup full-fat coconut milk
- 2 cups of blueberries
- 3 tbsp of gelatin
- 2 cups of ice
- Stevia

Instructions

Add everything except gelatin to the blender and turn it on. Blend until smooth, and then add gelatin. Blend again and enjoy.

21 Dairy And Egg Free Smoothie

(Ready in about 5 minutes | Serving 2 | Difficulty: Easy)

Per serving: Kcal 288, Fat: 17g, Net Carbs: 10g, Protein: 14g

Ingredients

- 1 cup coconut milk full fat
- 1 13 oz can of pumpkin organic
- 1/2 tsp of powder extract stevia
- 1/2 cup of water
- 1 tsp of organic cinnamon
- 2-3 cups of ice cubes
- 2 tbsp of golden flax ground
- 2 tbsp of hydrolysate gelatin
- 1 tsp of cinnamon

Instructions

Add everything to the blender and turn it on. Blend until smooth and enjoy.

22 Chai Smoothie

(Ready in about 5 minutes | Serving 1 | Difficulty: Easy)

Per serving: Kcal 726, Fat: 69g, Net Carbs: 20g, Protein: 5.5g

Ingredients

- 3/4 cup of coconut milk full-fat
- 1/2tsp of pumpkin spice
- 1 tsp of chai tea
- 3 tbsp of pumpkin puree
- 1 tsp of vanilla
- 1/2 frozen avocado

Instructions

Add everything except avocado to the blender and turn it on. Blend until smooth and add avocado. Blend again and enjoy.

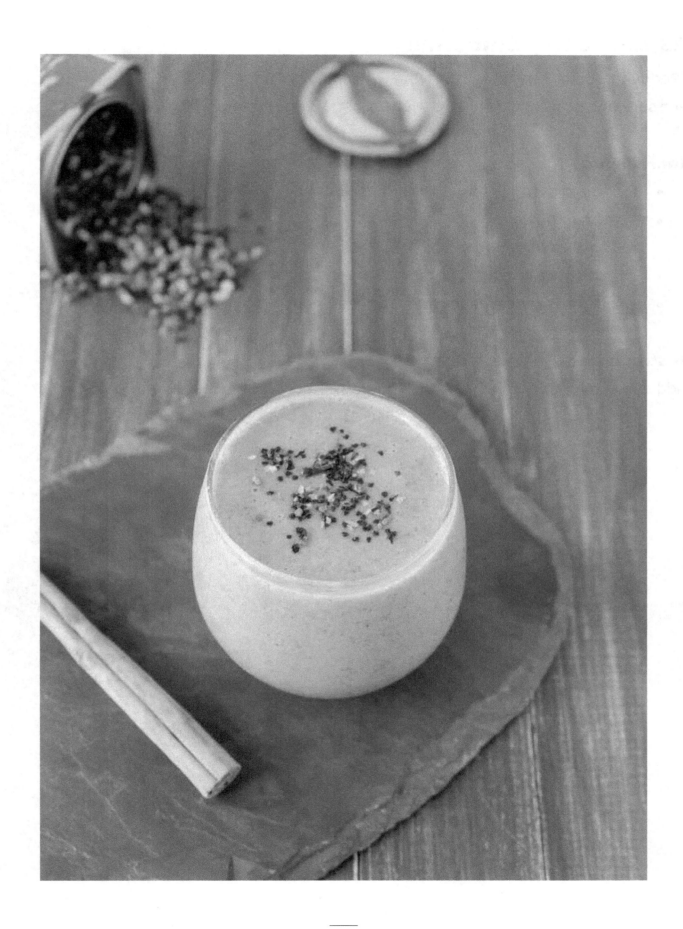

23 Raspberry Smoothie

(Ready in about 2 minutes | Serving 2 | Difficulty: Easy)

Per serving: Kcal 227, Fat: 20g, Net Carbs: 12.8g, Protein: 2.5g

Ingredients

- 1 ripe avocado pit removed and peeled
- 1 1/3 cup of water
- 2-3 tbsp of lemon juice
- 2 tbsp stevia extract
- 1/2 cup of frozen raspberries unsweetened

Instructions

Add everything to the blender and turn it on. Blend until smooth and enjoy.

24 Blueberry Smoothie

(Ready in about 5 minutes | Serving 1 | Difficulty: Easy)

Per serving: Kcal 215, Fat: 10g, Net Carbs: 7g, Protein: 23g

Ingredients

- 1 cup of Coconut Milk
- 1 tsp of Vanilla Extract
- 1/4 cup of Blueberries
- 1 tsp of MCT Oil

Instructions

Add everything to the blender and turn it on. Blend until smooth and enjoy.

25 Lime Strawberry Smoothie

(Ready in about 5 minutes | Serving 2 | Difficulty: Easy)

Per serving: Kcal 218, Fat: 13g, Net Carbs: 6g, Protein: 10g

Ingredients

- 1 can of coconut milk full fat
- 2 tbsp of MCT oil
- 8 ounces of frozen strawberries
- 1 tbsp freshly squeezed lime juice
- 1/4tsp of stevia
- 1 tbsp of lecithin powder

Instructions

Add everything to the blender and turn it on. Blend until smooth and enjoy.

26 Pie Smoothie

(Ready in about 5 minutes | Serving 2 | Difficulty: Easy)

Per serving: Kcal 753, Fat: 76g, Net Carbs: 20g, Protein: 14g

Ingredients

- 2 cups of coconut milk
- 4 tbsp of lime juice
- 2 tbsp of collagen
- 1/4 cup of macadamia nuts
- 1/2 medium-sized avocado
- 1 tbsp of erythritol
- 2 handfuls of spinach
- 2 tbsp of coconut butter
- One lime zest

Instructions

Add everything to the blender and turn it on. Blend until smooth and enjoy.

27 Base shake

(Ready in about 2 minutes | Serving 1 | Difficulty: Easy)

Per serving: Kcal 148, Fat: 10g, Net Carbs: 6g, Protein: 4g

Ingredients

- 1 cup almond milk unsweetened
- 1/2 cup of ice
- 2 tbsp of granulated sweetener
- 2 tbsp of almond butter

Instructions

Add everything to the blender and turn it on. Blend until smooth and enjoy.

28 Chocolate Shake

(Ready in about 2 minutes | Serving 1 | Difficulty: Easy)

Per serving: Kcal 148, Fat: 10g, Net Carbs: 6g, Protein: 4g

Ingredients

- 1/4 of avocado
- 2 tbsp of cocoa powder
- 1 cup almond milk unsweetened
- 1/2 cup of ice
- 2 tbsp of granulated sweetener
- 2 tbsp of almond butter

Instructions

Add everything to the blender and turn it on. Blend until smooth and enjoy.

29 Vanilla Shake

(Ready in about 2 minutes | Serving 1 | Difficulty: Easy)

Per serving: Kcal 148, Fat: 10g, Net Carbs: 6g, Protein: 4g

Ingredients

- 1/4 cup of frozen cauliflower
- 1 tsp of vanilla extract
- 1 cup almond milk unsweetened
- 1/2 cup of ice
- 2 tbsp of granulated sweetener
- 2 tbsp of almond butter

Instructions

Add everything to the blender and turn it on. Blend until smooth and enjoy.

30 Strawberry Shake

(Ready in about 2 minutes | Serving 1 | Difficulty: Easy)

Per serving: Kcal 148, Fat: 10g, Net Carbs: 6g, Protein: 4g

Ingredients

- 1/4 cup of frozen strawberries
- 1 tsp of vanilla extract
- 1 cup almond milk unsweetened
- 1/2 cup of ice
- 2 tbsp of granulated sweetener
- 2 tbsp of almond butter

Instructions

Add everything to the blender and turn it on. Blend until smooth and enjoy.

31 Blueberry Shake

(Ready in about 2 minutes | Serving 1 | Difficulty: Easy)

Per serving: Kcal 148, Fat: 10g, Net Carbs: 6g, Protein: 4g

Ingredients

- 1/4 cup of frozen blueberries
- 1 tsp of vanilla extract
- 1 cup almond milk unsweetened
- 1/2 cup of ice
- 2 tbsp of granulated sweetener
- 2 tbsp of almond butter

Instructions

Add everything to the blender and turn it on. Blend until smooth and enjoy.

32 Cinnamon Shake

(Ready in about 2 minutes | Serving 1 | Difficulty: Easy)

Per serving: Kcal 148, Fat: 10g, Net Carbs: 6g, Protein: 4g

Ingredients

- 1 tbsp of cinnamon
- 1 tsp of vanilla extract
- 1/4 cup of frozen cauliflower
- 1 cup almond milk unsweetened
- 1/2 cup of ice
- 2 tbsp of granulated sweetener
- 2 tbsp of almond butter

Instructions

Add everything to the blender and turn it on. Blend until smooth and enjoy.

33 Base Shake 2

(Ready in about 5 minutes | Serving 1 | Difficulty: Easy)

Ingredients

- 1 cup of Almond Milk
- 1 tbsp of Almond Butter
- 1/2 cup of ice
- 2 tbsp of Whipping Cream

Instructions

Add everything to the blender and turn it on. Blend until smooth and enjoy.

34 Lemon Shake

(Ready in about 5 minutes | Serving 1 | Difficulty: Easy)

Per serving: Kcal 354, Fat: 32.2g, Net Carbs: 11.3g, Protein: 8.1g

Ingredients

- 1/4 cup of Frozen Blueberries
- 5 drops of Liquid Stevia
- 1 tsp of Lemon Juice
- 2 tbsp of Cream Cheese
- 1/4 tsp of Lemon Zest
- 1 cup of Almond Milk
- 1 tbsp of Almond Butter
- 1/2 cup of ice
- 2 tbsp of Whipping Cream

Instructions

Add everything to the blender with base ingredients and turn it on. Blend until smooth and enjoy.

35 Pumpkin Spice Shake

(Ready in about 5 minutes | Serving 1 | Difficulty: Easy)

Per serving: Kcal 335, Fat: 30.6g, Net Carbs: 10.2g, Protein: 9.9g

Ingredients

- 2 tbsp of Pumpkin Puree
- 1 pinch of Grated Nutmeg
- 1/4 tsp of Pumpkin Pie Spice
- 1 tbsp of Almond Butter
- 5-10 drops of Liquid Stevia
- 1 cup of Almond Milk
- 1 tbsp of Almond Butter
- 1/2 cup of ice
- 2 tbsp of Whipping Cream

Instructions

Add everything with base ingredients to the blender and turn it on. Blend until smooth and enjoy.

36 Peanut Butter Shake

(Ready in about 5 minutes | Serving 1 | Difficulty: Easy)

Per serving: Kcal 419, Fat: 32.9g, Net Carbs: 10.9g, Protein: 23.5g

Ingredients

- 1/2 scoop of Protein Powder Chocolate
- 1 tbsp of Peanut Butter
- 1 tsp of Cocoa Powder Unsweetened
- 5-10 drops of Liquid Stevia
- 1 dark chocolate Square
- 1 cup of Almond Milk
- 1 tbsp of Almond Butter
- 1/2 cup of ice
- 2 tbsp of Whipping Cream

Instructions

Add everything to the blender except chocolate squares with base ingredients and turn it on. Blend until smooth and top with squares and enjoy.

37 Tiramisu Shake

(Ready in about 5 minutes | Serving 1 | Difficulty: Easy)

Per serving: Kcal 381, Fat: 35.8g, Net Carbs: 9.5g, Protein: 8.4g

Ingredients

- 1 Shot of coffee espresso
- 1 tsp of Cocoa Powder Unsweetened
- 2 tbsp of Cream Cheese
- 1 dark chocolate Square
- 5-10 drops of Liquid Stevia
- 1 cup of Almond Milk
- 1 tbsp of Almond Butter
- 1/2 cup of ice
- 2 tbsp of Whipping Cream

Instructions

Add everything to the blender except chocolate squares with base ingredients and turn it on. Blend until smooth and enjoy.

38 Birthday Cake

(Ready in about 5 minutes | Serving 1 | Difficulty: Easy)

Per serving: Kcal 414, Fat: 36.2g, Net Carbs: 8g, Protein: 18.1g

Ingredients

- 1/2 scoop of Protein Powder Vanilla
- 1 tsp of Sprinkles Sugar-Free
- 1/4 tsp of Almond extract
- 1 tbsp of Melted Butter
- 5-10 drops of Liquid Stevia
- 1 cup of Almond Milk
- 1 tbsp of Almond Butter
- 1/2 cup of ice
- 2 tbsp of Whipping Cream

Instructions

Add everything to the blender except half amount of sprinkles with base ingredients and turn it on. Blend until smooth and top with sprinkles and enjoy.

39 Shamrock Shake

(Ready in about 5 minutes | Serving 1 | Difficulty: Easy)
Per serving: Kcal 259, Fat: 14g, Net Carbs: 7g, Protein: 26g

Ingredients

- 1/2 medium-sized avocado
- 1 scoop of protein powder vanilla
- 1/2 cup of almond
- 8 ice cubes
- ⅛ tsp of peppermint extract
- 5 drops of natural food coloring green
- 1 tbsp of chocolate chips dark

Instructions

Add everything except chocolate chips to the blender and turn it on. Blend until smooth and top using chocolate chips and enjoy.

40 Coconut Shake

(Ready in about 5 minutes | Serving 2 | Difficulty: Easy)

Per serving: Kcal 222, Fat: 23.1g, Net Carbs: 5.4g, Protein: 2.5g

Ingredients

- 4 oz full-fat coconut cream
- 8 oz almond
- 1/2 tbsp of almond butter
- 2 tbsp of coconut oil
- Sea salt
- 2 tbsp of cocoa powder

Instructions

Add everything to the blender and turn it on. Blend until smooth and enjoy.

41 Peppermint Milkshake

(Ready in about 5 minutes | Serving 1 | Difficulty: Easy)

Per serving: Kcal 436, Fat: 42g, Net Carbs: 15g, Protein: 5g

Ingredients

- 8 ounces of coconut cream
- 1/4 cup of organic spinach
- 2 tbsp of cocoa powder
- 1/2 tsp of stevia glycerite
- 2 drops of peppermint extract
- 1 cup of almond milk unsweetened
- 1 pinch of Himalayan salt

Instructions

Add everything to the blender and turn it on. Blend until smooth and enjoy.

42 Strawberry Milkshake

(Ready in about 5 minutes | Serving 1 | Difficulty: Easy)

Per serving: Kcal 276, Fat: 27.4g, Net Carbs: 6.4g, Protein: 2.5g

Ingredients

- 1/4 cup of coconut milk
- 1 tbsp of MCT oil
- 1/2 cup of strawberries
- 3/4 cup of almond milk unsweetened
- 1/2 tsp of vanilla extract sugar-free

Instructions

Add everything to the blender and turn it on. Blend until smooth and enjoy.

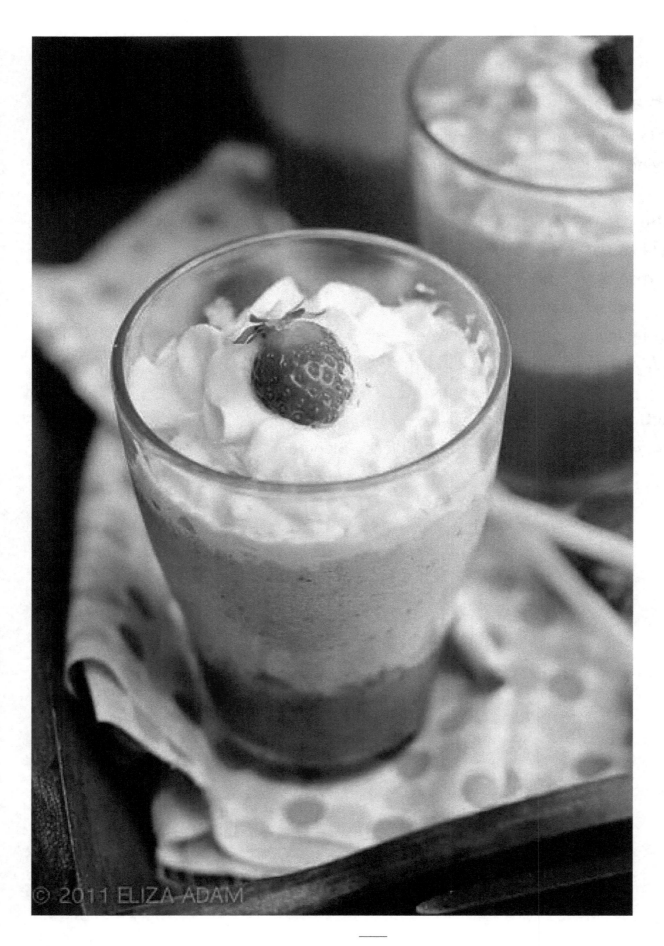

43 Blackberry Shake

(Ready in about 3 minutes | Serving 1 | Difficulty: Easy)

Per serving: Kcal 364, Fat: 34g, Net Carbs: 4.8g, Protein: 2.6g

Ingredients

- 7 cubes of ice
- 2 tbsp of MCT oil
- 1/4 cup of blackberries
- 1 cup of coconut milk unsweetened
- 2 tbsp of cocoa powder
- 1/4tsp of xanthan gum
- 12 drops of liquid stevia

Instructions

Add everything to the blender and turn it on. Blend until smooth and enjoy.

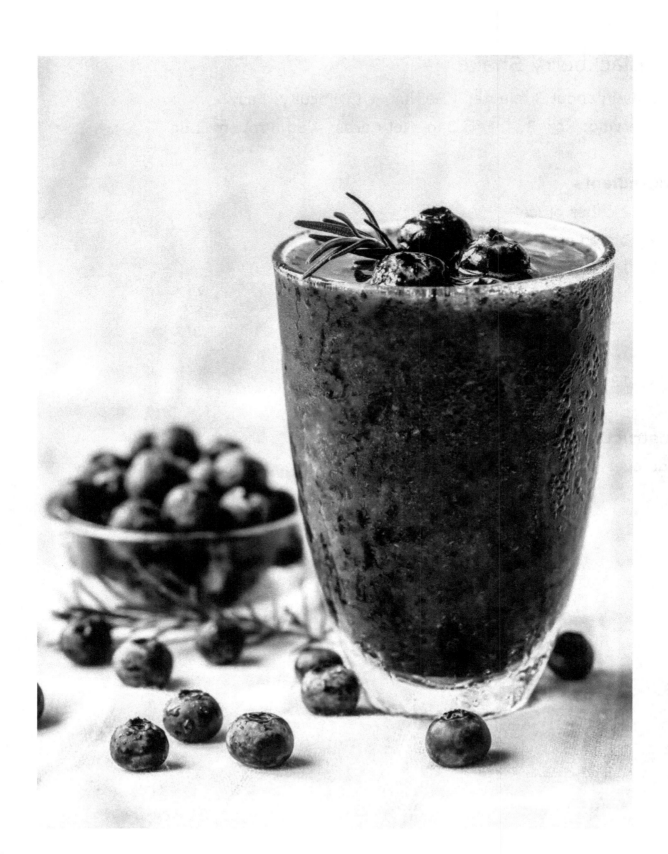

44 Frozen Berry Shake

(Ready in about 5 minutes | Serving 1 | Difficulty: Easy)

Per serving: Kcal 400, Fat: 41g, Net Carbs: 6.7g, Protein: 4g

Ingredients

- 1/3 cup of coconut milk
- Ice cubes
- 1/2 cup of frozen berries
- 1/2 cup of water
- 1 tbsp of MCT oil

Instructions

Place coconut milk in the fridge overnight to cream it. Extract solidified milk from the can and add the rest of the ingredients to the blender and turn it on. Blend until smooth and enjoy.

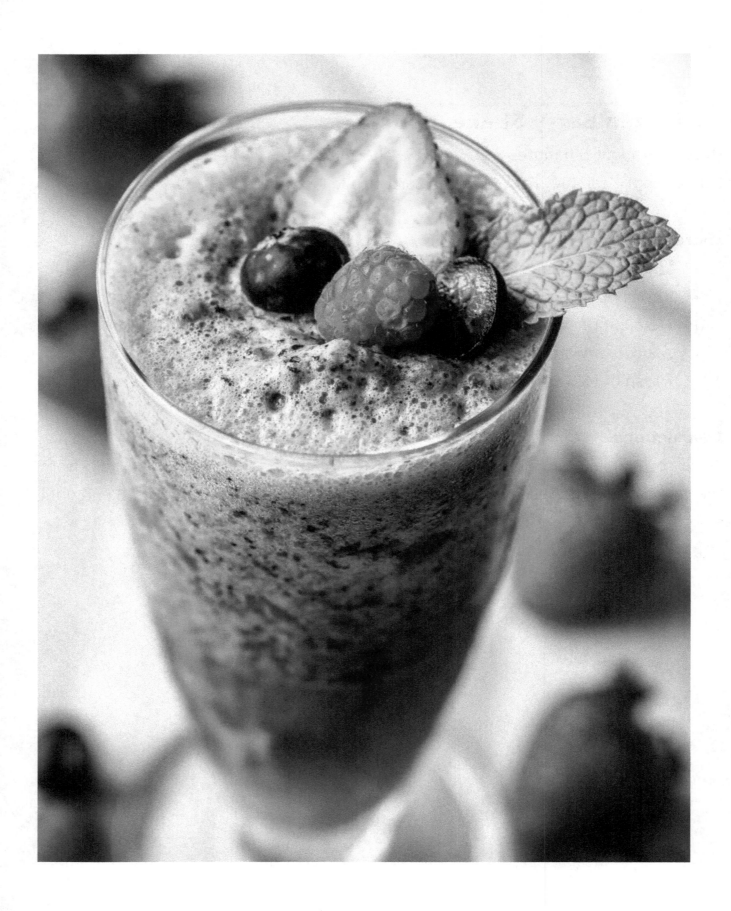

45 Cookies Milkshake

(Ready in about 15 minutes | Serving 2 | Difficulty: Easy)

Per serving: Kcal 546, Fat: 50g, Net Carbs: 8g, Protein: 5g

Ingredients

For crumbs

- 1 tbsp of butter melted
- 30 g of almond flour
- 1-2 tbsp of powdered erythritol
- 6 g of cocoa powder
- Kosher salt

For milkshake

- 1/4 cup of almond milk unsweetened
- 2 cups of ice cream vanilla

Instructions

For crumbs

Toast flour in a pan for around 4 minutes. Transfer to a bowl and mix with the rest of the oreo ingredients. Place in freezer.

For milkshake

Add everything with the half-crumbs mixture to the blender and turn it on. Blend until smooth and add the rest of the crumbs and enjoy.

46 Batter Milkshake

(Ready in about 2 minutes | Serving 1 | Difficulty: Easy)

Per serving: Kcal 480, Fat: 46.4g, Net Carbs: 7.95g, Protein: 15.98g

Ingredients

- 1/2 cup of almond milk
- 1/4 cup of crushed ice
- 1/4 cup of coconut milk full fat
- 50g of ground almonds
- 7 drops of liquid stevia
- 1 tsp of coconut oil
- 1/4 tsp of vanilla powder

Instructions

Add everything to the blender and turn it on. Blend until smooth and enjoy.

47 Cookie Milkshake

(Ready in about 1 hour 10 minutes | Serving 1 | Difficulty: Easy)

Per serving: Kcal 120, Fat: 2.5g, Net Carbs: 25g, Protein: 2g

Ingredients

- 3 cups of milk
- 1/2 tsp of vanilla extract
- 1/4 tsp of baking soda
- 1 frozen banana
- 1/4 tsp of tartar cream

Instructions

Add everything to the blender and turn it on. Blend until smooth and enjoy.

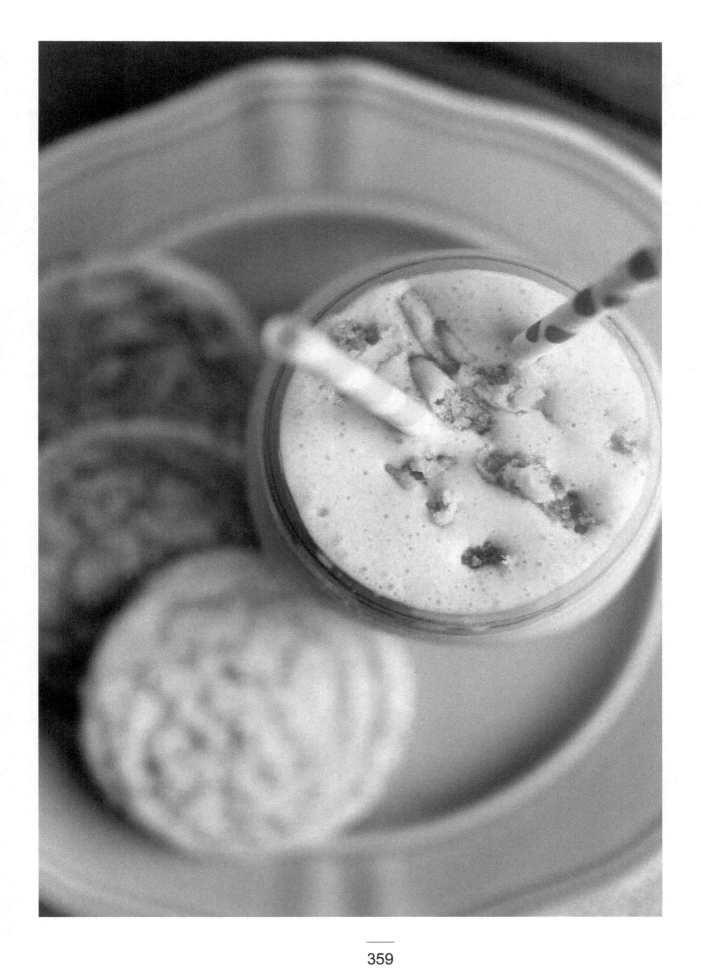

48 Almond Butter Shake

(Ready in about 2 minutes | Serving 1 | Difficulty: Easy)

Per serving: Kcal 326, Fat: 27g, Net Carbs: 11g, Protein: 19g

Ingredients

- 1 1/2 cups of nut milk unsweetened
- 2 Tbsp of almond butter
- 1/8 tsp of salt
- 1 scoop of collagen peptides
- 2 Tbsp of golden flax meal
- 15 drops of liquid stevia
- 1/2 tsp of cinnamon
- 1/8 tsp of almond extract
- 6 ice cubes

Instructions

Add everything to the blender and turn it on. Blend until smooth and enjoy.

49 Turmeric Milkshake

(Ready in about 5 minutes | Serving 1 | Difficulty: Easy)

Per serving: Kcal 351, Fat: 35.2g, Net Carbs: 6.9g, Protein: 1.6g

Ingredients

- 375 ml of coconut milk
- 3/4 tsp of turmeric powder
- Himalayan salt
- 2 tbsp of coconut oil
- 1/2 tsp of ginger powder
- 1/4 tsp of vanilla
- 1/4 tsp of cinnamon
- granulated sweetener
- 2 ice cubes

Instructions

Add everything to the blender and turn it on. Blend until smooth and enjoy.

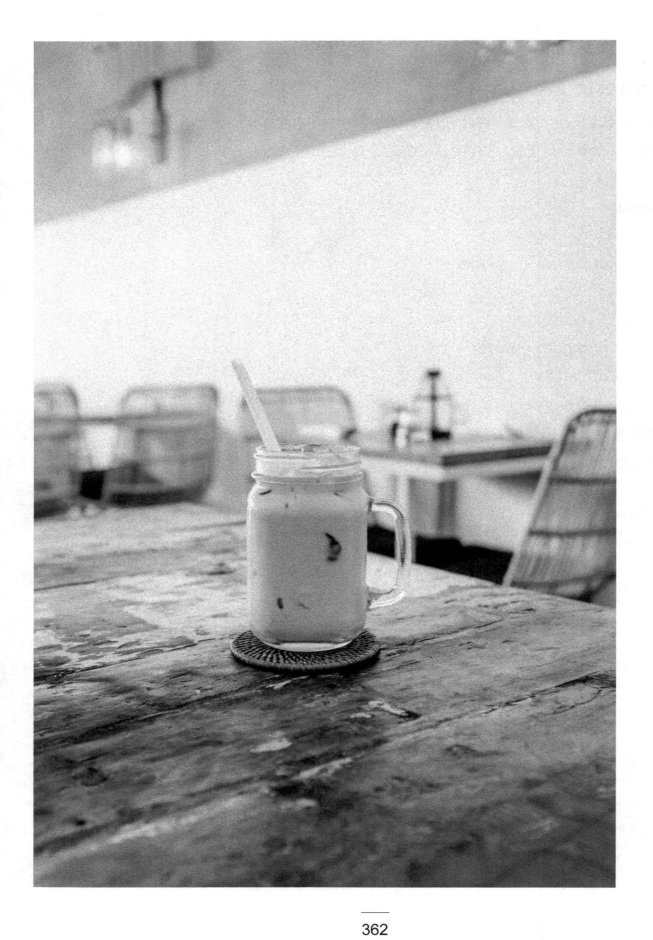

50 Cinnamon Roll Shake

(Ready in about 5 minutes | Serving 1 | Difficulty: Easy)

Per serving: Kcal 386, Fat: 17g, Net Carbs: 8g, Protein: 12g

Ingredients

- 1 cup of almond milk
- 1 tsp of cinnamon
- 2 Tbsp of almond butter
- 1/4 tsp of vanilla
- 1/4 cup of ice cubes
- 1 Tbsp of Liquid Sweetener
- 1 scoop of Powdered Collagen
- 1 dash of nutmeg

Instructions

Add everything to the blender and turn it on. Blend until smooth and enjoy.

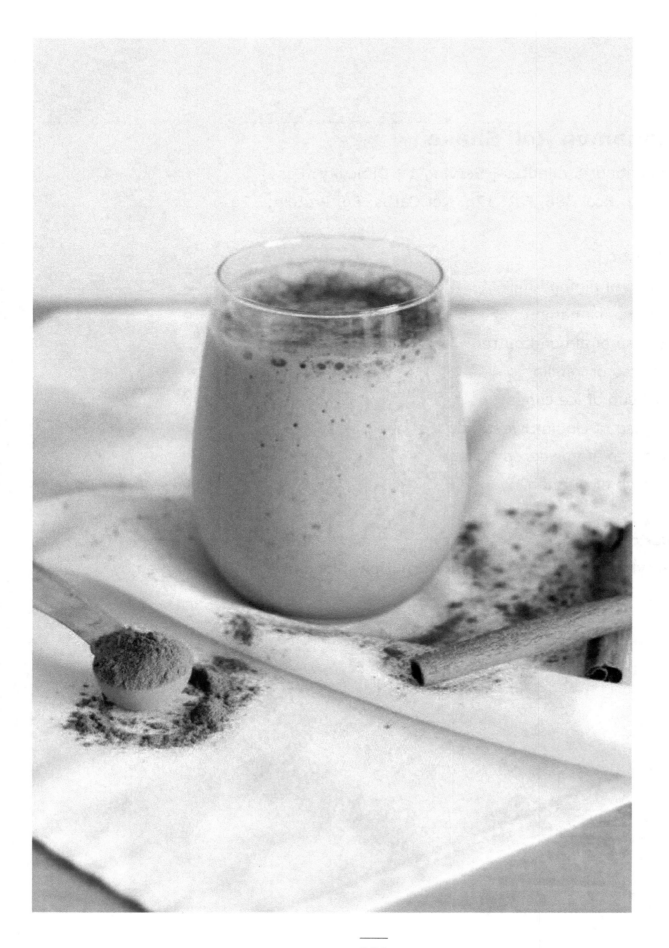

51 Hot Chocolate Shake

(Ready in about 8 minutes | Serving 4 | Difficulty: Easy)

Per serving: Kcal 770, Fat: 40g, Net Carbs: 89, Protein: 12g

Ingredients

- 1 1/2 cups of almond milk unsweetened
- 1 tsp of liquid stevia
- 1/2 cup of protein powder chocolate
- 3 ounces of chocolate chopped
- 1/2 tsp of peppermint extract
- 2 cups of ice

Instructions

Add everything to the blender and turn it on. Blend until smooth and enjoy.

Chocolate Milkshake

©fullscoops

www.fullscoops.net

52 Bacon Milkshake

(Ready in about 5 minutes | Serving 1 | Difficulty: Easy)

Per serving: Kcal 386, Fat: 17g, Net Carbs: 8g, Protein: 12g

The shake

- 6 Tbsp of heavy cream
- 4 Tbsp of bacon fat
- 4 Tbsp of maple syrup
- 10 scoops of ice cream vanilla

The syrup

- 4 Tbsp of replacement brown sugar
- 4 Tbsp of cocoa
- 4 Tbsp of butter

The cream

- 1/4 tsp of maple extract
- 1 cup of white cream
- 1/4 cup of sweetener

Instructions

Whip maple extract, sweetener and heavy cream in a bowl for around 5 minutes. Add the rest of the ingredients to the blender and turn it on. Blend until smooth and top with whipped cream. Heat syrup ingredients in the microwave for around 20 seconds and drizzle on shake.

53 Homemade Milk

(Ready in about 9Hrs 5 minutes | Serving 4 | Difficulty: medium)
Per serving: Kcal 176, Fat: 13g, Net Carbs: 11.5g, Protein: 5.7g

Ingredients

- ⅓ cup of skin-on, raw almonds
- ⅓ cup of rolled oats
- 1 tbsp. whole flax seeds
- 4 cup of filtered water, divided
- ⅓ cup of cashews

Directions

- In a large mixing bowl, add the almonds, cashews, and oats and fill with 2 cups of water. Allow at least eight hours to absorb in the refrigerator.
- Remove from the refrigerator and stir in the flax seeds. Allow 1 hour for the flax seeds to interact with water and the mixture to hit room temperature.
- Blend until smooth and creamy in a blender. Allow for five-minute to rest. Add the last two cups of filtered water. Blend till smooth, creamy, and well mixed. Using a fine-mesh sieve, filter the pulp. You should eat it straight away or keep it in the fridge for up to a week, until using, giving it a good shake.

54 Vanilla Almond Shake

(Ready in about 5 minutes | Serving 1 | Difficulty: Easy)

Per serving: Kcal 176, Fat: 13g, Net Carbs: 11.5g, Protein: 5.7g

Ingredients

- 1 tbsp. sliced almonds
- ½ cup of ice
- 1 cup of water
- 1 tsp. sugar-free, Fats-free, vanilla pudding mix
- ⅔ cup of powdered milk, non-Fat

Directions

- Blend ice, 1/4 cup water, and almonds in a blender till the almonds are pulverized. Add the remaining powdered milk, pudding mix, and water, then continue blending till smooth.

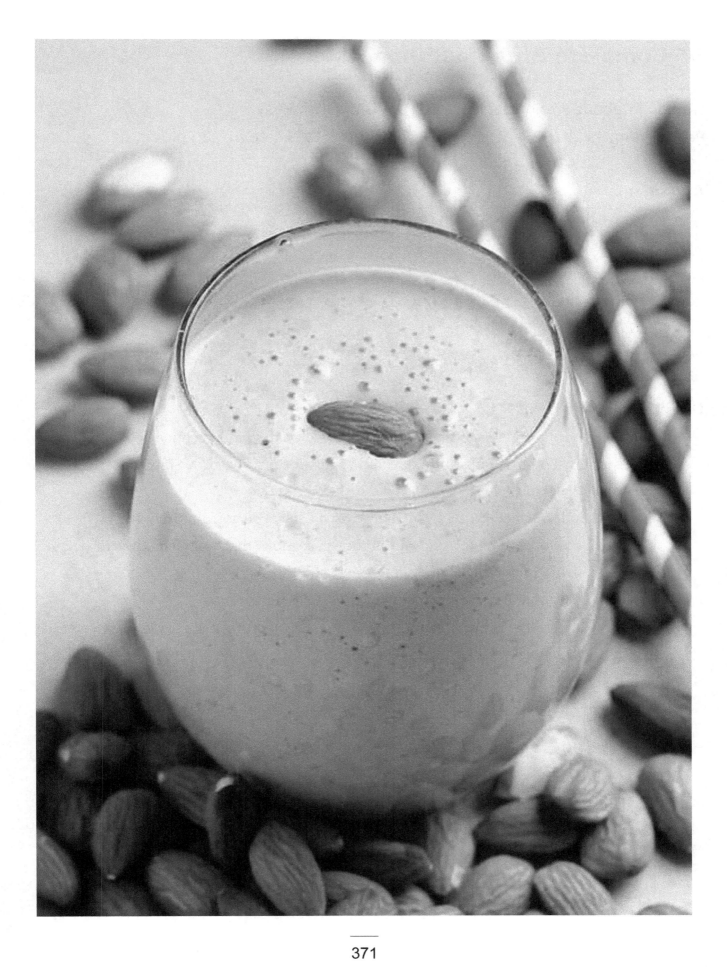

55 Complete Breakfast Smoothie

(Ready in about 5 minutes | Serving 1 | Difficulty: Easy)

Per serving: Kcal 362, Fat: 9.4g, Net Carbs:45.1g, Protein: 28.2g

Ingredients

- ½ cup of berries, mixed frozen
- ¼ cup of Greek yogurt
- ¼ cup of oats, steel-cut
- ¼ cup of water
- 1 scoop of protein powder
- 1 tsp of honey

Directions

- In a processor, mix berries, yogurt, protein powder, oats, water, & honey until smooth.
- Chef's Notes: You may substitute flavored yogurt for plain yogurt. Simply keep an eye on the sugar level while you're monitoring the glucose intake.
- This is a good source of protein which fiber & will keep you going until lunch.
- Utilize whichever sweetener you want in the proportions that complement your palate. In this dish, sugar, Splenda(R), honey, and stevia all fit well.
- If you like, you may also use a protein powder that is flavored.
- You will adjust the berry mix to your preference. In every mix, blend strawberries, raspberries, blueberries, blackberries, & cherries.

56 Grapefruit, Lime & Mint Yogurt Parfait

(Ready in about 15 minutes | Serving 6 | Difficulty: Easy)

Per serving: Kcal 207, Fat: 3g, Net Carbs:39g, Protein: 10g

Ingredients

- 4 large grapefruit red
- 4 cups of plain yogurt reduced fat
- 2 tsp lime zest grated
- 2 tbsp lime juice
- 3 tbsp honey
- mint leaves, Torn fresh

Directions:

- Every grapefruit should have a tiny slice cut from the top & bottom; put fruit upright over the cutting board. Remove the outer membrane and peel from the grapefruit using a knife. Remove fruit by cutting along the surface of each segment.
- Combine lime zest, yogurt, and juice in a mixing cup. In six parfait glasses, layer grapefruit & yogurt mixture. Repetition of layers. Drizzle honey over the top; garnish with mint.

Conclusion

A keto diet may be a healthier option for certain people, although the amount of fat, carbohydrates, and protein prescribed varies from person to person. If you have diabetes, talk to the doctor before starting the diet because it would almost certainly need prescription changes and stronger blood sugar regulation. Are you taking drugs for high blood pressure? Before starting a keto diet again, talk to the doctor. If you're breastfeeding, you shouldn't follow a ketogenic diet. Be mindful that limiting carbs will render you irritable, hungry, and sleepy, among other things. However, this may be a one-time occurrence. Keep in mind that you can eat a balanced diet in order to obtain all of the vitamins and minerals you need. A sufficient amount of fiber is also needed. When the body begins to derive energy from accumulated fat rather than glucose, it is said to be in ketosis. Several trials have shown the powerful weight-loss benefits of a low-carb, or keto, diet. This diet, on the other hand, can be difficult to stick to and can exacerbate health issues in individuals who have certain disorders, such as diabetes type 1. The keto diet is suitable for the majority of citizens. Nonetheless, all major dietary modifications should be discussed with a dietitian or doctor. This is essentially the case with people who have inherent conditions. The keto diet may be an effective therapy for people with drug-resistant epilepsy. Though the diet may be beneficial to people of any age, teenagers, people over 50, and babies can profit the most because they can easily stick to it. Modified keto diets, such as the revised Atkins diet or the low-glycemic index diet, are safer for adolescents and adults. A health care worker should keep a careful eye on someone who is taking a keto diet as a treatment. A doctor and dietitian will maintain track of a person's progress, administer drugs, and test for side effects. The body absorbs fat and protein differently than it does carbohydrates. Carbohydrates have a high insulin reaction. The protein sensitivity to insulin is mild, and the quick insulin response is negligible. Insulin is a fat-producing and fat-conserving enzyme. If you wish to lose weight, consume as many eggs, chickens, fish, and birds as you want, satiate yourself with the fat, and then eat every vegetable that grows on the ground. Butter and coconut oil can be used instead of processed synthetic seed oils. You may be either a sugar or a fat burner, but not both.

CPSIA information can be obtained
at www.ICGtesting.com
Printed in the USA
LVHW050537120521
687183LV00015B/1595